MAGGIE BROSNAN
3226 GARDENDALE DRIVE
SAN JOSE, CALIFORNIA 95118
(408) 264-6637

D0787677

CREATING BODY COVERINGS

1

2

3

4

5

6

7

8

9

CREATING
BODY COVERINGS

JEAN RAY LAURY
JOYCE AIKEN

Photographs by Cam Smith

 VAN NOSTRAND REINHOLD COMPANY
NEW YORK CINCINNATI TORONTO LONDON MELBOURNE

Van Nostrand Reinhold Company Regional Offices:
New York Cincinnati Chicago Millbrae Dallas

Van Nostrand Reinhold Company International
Offices:
London Toronto Melbourne

Library of Congress Catalog Card Number 73-1631

ISBN 0 442-24692-7 (pbk.)

ISBN 0 442-24698-6

Published by Van Nostrand Reinhold Company
450 West 33rd Street, New York, N.Y. 10001
Published simultaneously in Canada by
Van Nostrand Reinhold Limited

16 15 14 13 12 11 10 9 8 7 6 5 4 3 2 1

Library of Congress Cataloging in Publication Data

Laury, Jean Ray.
  Creating body coverings.

  1. Clothing and dress. 2. Fancy work. 3. Decora-
tion and ornament. I. Aiken, Joyce, joint author.
II. Title.
TT507.L34   746.9'2   73-1631
ISBN 0-442-24698-6
ISBN 0-442-24692-7 (pbk.)

I-1. Hand-knit socks with hearts. By Ritva Vehkasalo, Helsinki, Finland.

C-1. A simply cut pullover of white felt is appliquéd in yellow. Gold is inserted between the layers for a cut-through effect, and all edges are whipstitched. By Jean Ray Laury, Clovis, Calif.

C-2. After piecing together a few colors of Mexican cotton, the shirt parts are cut. Then bands of fabric and ribbons are added before the parts are joined. When the assembly is complete, velveteen appliqués are added. By Jean Ray Laury.

C-3. Fabric designer Elizabeth Freeman, of Beverly Hills, Calif., is well known for her stitch-and-dye panels. Using that technique, she decorated this wedding shirt with rainbow-colored stars.

C-4. Doilies and lace are combined with grosgrain ribbons, velvet ribbons, colored cotton fabrics, and simple appliqué in a summer shirt. By Jean Ray Laury.

C-5. Designer Norman Laliberté of Brewster, N. Y. uses a permanent marking pen and dye to paint elaborately and decorate this body mask. The linear pattern and rich detail are reminiscent of his well-known banners.

C-6. An old-fashioned "long-John" underwear shirt in batik uses a celestial pattern of purples. By a San Francisco street artist.

C-7. A rainbow of color travels across a caftan designed and modeled by Elizabeth Freeman. Her technique of stitch-and-dye requires patience and exactness.

C-8. Ski cape of red felt with wine felt appliqués. The flaps are made separately and then machine stitched under the hem edge. Slots in the front allow for easy arm movement. By Jean Ray Laury.

C-9. Army fatigue jackets are favorites among teen-agers. This one is embellished with embroidery and with patches from surplus stores, ski shops, and old scout uniforms. By Liz Laury, Clovis, Calif.

To Stan and Howard, who will be two of the best-dressed men in rural Clovis, just as soon as we get their Levis patched.

With our warmest thanks to:
Cam Smith, who happily tramped with camera
   gear through snow, water, weeds, and traffic
   to photograph so much of the work in this book.
Gayle Smalley for her careful photographing of
   the many details shown.
Bev O'Neal, our girl Friday (seven days a week).

And special thanks to the talented designers who so generously shared their magic and humor and beautiful creations.

I-2. Quilted patchwork vest. By Elsa Brown, Ridgefield, Conn.

Contents

I-3. Necktie. By Susan Morrison, Reno, Nev.

Introduction

Body coverings are a kind of celebration. They make festive occasions of dinners or parties, or of just joining a friend for coffee. The way you dress can greatly compliment your guests or friends in that you provide them with the visual pleasures of your creative efforts. Clothing offers a means of sharing some of the joy you may feel in creative needlework.

When we cover our bodies with clothing in the morning, which most of us do each day, we describe ourselves to other people. We give them clues and shortcuts as to who we are and what we do. The pinstriped business suit, a studded motorcycle jacket, outdated thrift-shop garments, or blue denims all help to identify us. Our clothes show, to some extent, what we are, or what we would like to be, or sometimes pretend to be. They invite fantasy and let us perform the role which we select for ourselves.

Clothing needs vary from day to day and from one role to another. Daily activities place restrictions on what you wear. To supervise a soccer game, or take the Cub Scouts to the junior museum, you need clothing different from that of the bank teller or the gardener. What you would wear to throw pots on the potter's wheel is probably not the same thing you would wear to the junior-high faculty meeting. But for free time—the after-work hours, weekends, time at home—anyone is free to become whatever

he would like to be, or whatever he is.

Sometimes you hide yourself with clothing. You hope to make yourself inconspicuous, to go unnoticed, to be anonymous. What is inconspicuous varies, of course. What may conceal you while birdwatching would make you stand out at a formal occasion. What would go unnoticed at the beach would not at an office-retirement dinner. Being inconspicuous involves blending into what is accepted, or standard, and dressing appropriately to the place or the occasion. It means to visually melt, or blend, into the surroundings. The con man at the card table must look like his intended victims to be accepted by them. A writer interviewing farm workers would have better rapport if he didn't wear a hat or a bow tie.

Many painters, stitchers, and sculptors over the country are becoming interested in taking their work beyond the confines of gallery walls. Instead of having viewers see their work only within the boundaries of a room, these artists also like to wear their work among their friends, adapting their creative efforts to the things they wear. Homemakers everywhere are tired of wearing what fashions dictate and seem, at last, to be rebellious enough to make up their own minds about their clothing. Students have made some innovative changes in clothing, rejecting the ideas that certain things are right, or correct, and thus leading to an enjoyment of the unconventional. This may be partially just a shift to a new style, but at least it is an accepting and open style, which enjoys the absurd and the beautiful, the exotic as well as the recycled.

1-4. Worn blue jeans overalls are given a new life in this embroidered jumper. Back overall straps are brought around to the front as a new bib top, decorated with a doily. The leg seams, split and sewn together, make a long skirt. More yarn embroidery was added along skirt seams by designer Bea Slater, Clovis, Calif.

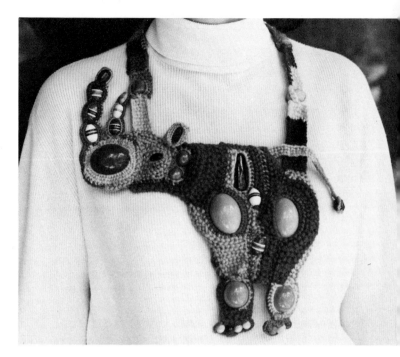

I-5. Rhinoceros necklace, crocheted in brilliant yarns, is adorned with shiny wooden beads. By Ben Sheppard, Seattle, Wash.

I-6. A girl's drawings of horses provided the basis for an appliquéd halter top. Embroidery lines are being added for detail. Designed by Lizabeth Laury.

Mass production has made reasonable, serviceable clothing available to almost everyone. But it has also deprived the clothing of any personal character. To feel unique, or special, it is important to do something to personalize, or individualize, the garment.

Because most clothing is fabric, whether natural or synthetic, an obvious means of personalizing is through sewing. Appliqué and embroidery are probably the best known ways to add individuality to clothing. These may be added to the surface of ready-made clothes, or clothes made from yardage. Printing, painting, dyeing, or batiking saturates the fabric with color. And, finally, fabric may be formed by crocheting, knitting, weaving, or by macramé so that the garment and the decorative effect emerge together.

Covering your body is not like covering your walls, since you're never committed for a very long time. You don't have to take it all too seriously, since it is impermanent and readily changed.

One essential aspect of clothing, if you are to be yourself, is comfort. Physical comfort alone is not enough, since we know that people will endure excruciating discomfort if the clothing allows them to appear to be what they visualize, or accept, as most desirable. But even while achieving this ideal, it is impossible to be at home with yourself while in physical discomfort. You must also be comfortable psychologically in feeling that the clothes are a logical, acceptable, compatible extension of yourself. You must feel right in them. Clothes must reflect at least some aspect of what you consider the "real you."

Many people who are uninterested in clothes don't wish to contend with the distracting nature of ex-traordinary, or beautiful, clothes. They find these clothes an interference; and clothes *can* interfere. These people often prefer to let conversation, action, and communication reveal their own personalities. Still other people count on clothes to make up for attributes which they may lack. Furs, diamonds, or designer signatures are easily recognized as ways in which some wearers attempt to tell us who they are. But between these extremes there is a whole world of possibilities.

There are extravagantly beautiful garments of ceremonial import. There are the joyous, simple, everyday clothes which are delightful and amusing to see or wear. These are the body coverings which may transport both wearer and viewer, casting a spell over a room or over a group, and heightening the visual delights and pleasures of just being there.

This book is devoted to the simple ways in which any of you can personalize your clothes. The methods are basic and the results are varied. A few of the designers whose works are shown pursue their crafts as full-time professionals. But most of the clothes are made by people with no special talents or skills—just an intrigue with the decorative possibilities and a willingness to share them.

The purpose of this book is to inspire and to encourage the reader and to open to him the creative possibilities of clothing design. Some of the clothes are directed towards an ecological recycling of old clothes, or non-clothes—adapting, changing, and re-using the discards. Many require new materials and simple construction methods. All involve a wholesome, humorous, open, and very human approach to clothing and body coverings.

1. Embroidery

Exquisite detail and delicate color are easily added to clothing by means of embroidery. It is much like drawing in that your needle leaves a trail of small lines, patterns, or doodles. Embroidery is great for the beginner. Only the simplest stitches need be used, and often the fewest are the most effective. Many examples of very easy embroidery are included. For the accomplished embroiderer, the challenges of needlework on clothing are unending.

THE T-SHIRT

The most mundane articles of clothing, highlighted with embroidery, become special. T-shirts become three-dimensional drawings as the embroidery takes its form over the body. While embroidery may be worked flat, it assumes its full shape only when it is worn.

Bets Barnard salvaged her son's T-shirt on its way to the ragbag and transformed it with her stitching. She particularly enjoys turning a plain garment into something unique, as is evident in Figure 1-1 and in Figure C-26. Her embroidery here consists of one

Text continues on p. 16

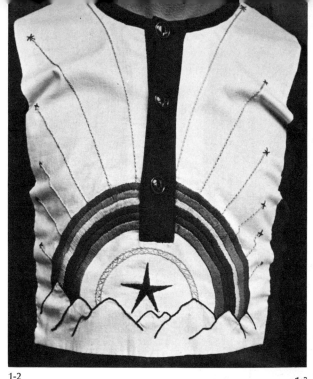

1-2

1-3

1-1. "Tulip Shirt." Chain stitches, sewn with embroidery floss, fill the solid areas of color in these flowers. Care should be taken that the embroidery stitches are not pulled so tightly that they pucker the T-shirt material. By Bets Barnard.

1-2. "Rainbow T-Shirt." A combination of outline and chain stitches with embroidery floss is used in this T-shirt, designed and sewn by John Jensen, Fresno, Calif.

1-3. "Flowers." An embroidered garland of pretty flowers encircles the neckline of this cotton shirt. The effect of this profusion of blossoms belies the simplicity of the stitches. By Joanne Derr.

1-4. Butterflies and flowers grow delicately around the cuffs and up the side seams of blue denim pants, made to match the garland in the preceding illustration. By Joanne Derr.

1-5. Embroidery stitches form a sampler on a blue denim work shirt. By Jody House.

1-6. Guitars embellish the yoke of a western denim shirt. Embroidery is worked solid, using an embroidery hoop. By Mimi Shimmin, San Francisco, Calif.

1-7. Marilyn Bishop designed the simple embroidery used on ready-made vests. The embroidery on her own shirt was designed by Malcomb Lubliner. Both are from Los Angeles, Calif.

1-8. Detail, with more stitches of the sampler above.

1-9. Chain stitches were used in the design which covers the entire back panel of a shirt. Designed and sewn by John Reyburn, Los Angeles, who is wearing his own work.

1-10. "Circles." A panel of pale yellow knit cotton, set into the brown T-shirt, shows off the embroidery stitches and French knots. By Joanne Derr.

1-11

1-11. Small mica mirrors, securely held by embroidery stitches, adorn the collar, cuffs, and pocket of a wrangler shirt. By Jean Simpson.

1-12. Detail of Jean Simpson's mirror embroidery on a dress of homespun cotton fabric.

1-12

simple stitch—the chain stitch—using regular dime-store, or department-store, embroidery floss. The areas of solid color are offset with a few lazy daisies, added last to fill in an area around the tulips.

The T-shirts in Figures 1-2, 1-3, and 1-10 all began as ordinary, inexpensive, cotton shirts. Embroidered, they are extraordinary.

BLUE DENIMS

Blue denim shirts offer a great beginning for embroidery. The material is soft in color and texture, and the unpretentious nature of the shirt makes it a natural. Jody House starts her stitchery students off on a beginning embroidery project which uses some portions of the shirt. Figures 1-5 and 1-8 show these shirt "samplers."

Two other denim work shirts glorify the blue-collar costume in Figures 1-6 and 1-9.

MIRROR, MIRROR

Mirrors are the focal point in embroidery by Jean Simpson. Stitches surround each mirror to hold it in place and to frame the shiny fragment of light. Examples in Figures 1-11 and 1-12 show the Cretan stitch, embellished with French knots or fly stitch. See Figure C-25 (page 37). Jean reminds anyone starting to be sure to use heavy enough fabric so that it can hold the weight of the mirrors. Phyllis Hall uses a similar stitch-over-mirror approach in her vest, Figure 1-13.

CROSS-STITCH

June Moes has used a unique means of applying cross-stitch to clothing as shown in Figures 1-19 and 1-20. She did not invent or devise the method, but she adapted it to use on her clothes. Using either cross-stitch patterns or her own designs, she first binds the piece of canvas with masking tape and then bastes the printed canvas to the shirt. She then proceeds with the cross-stitch, sewing through the fabric. The work is neater and there is less puckering if the "punch" method is used rather than the "sewing" method. This work in progress can be seen in Figure 1-21. In the white blouse, Figure 1-19, June used a 12/1 cross-stitch canvas, which she felt was a little small. A size 10/1 or 8/1 would be preferable. The numbers refer to how many openings, or stitches, are used to go across, or down, one inch of canvas. A size 10/1 has ten openings across and ten openings down, making 100 openings in a square inch of canvas. That means that 100 stitches will be required to fill that area solid with stitches. When working on a white shirt, June recommends that you paint the canvas yellow, or it will be difficult to see white on a white background. For her stitches, she uses 6 strands of cotton embroidery floss on the 8/1 canvas, 4 strands on the 10/1 canvas, and 3 strands on the 12/1 canvas.

When the cross-stitch on the canvas is complete, the masking tape is cut away from the edge. Canvas and blouse are dampened, and each thread of the original canvas is drawn out. Then you "watch your design come alive," according to June. This leaves only the cross-stitches on the shirt fabric.

As you go through the color photographs, you will will see many other examples, both traditional and contemporary, of embroidery for clothing. Among

Text continues on p. 22

1-13. Mirror-embroidered vest. By Phyllis Hall, Los Angeles, Calif.

1-14. A simple cotton shirt is made special with sampler stitches around the neck and a trailing vine of embroidery down the sleeve. By Cecilia Christensen, Palo Alto, Calif.

1-15 and 16. This dress was made and embroidered to go with a belt which the designer received as a gift. Using the same motif, she embroidered in gold around the neck and down an opening at the side of the dress. By Joanne Derr.

1-13

1-14

1-15

1-16

C-10. *Navajo velvet dress, designed by Jo Diggs of Corrales, N. Mex., combines various textures and materials to contrast with, and complement, the areas of exposed skin.*

C-11. *"Traveling Cloak." Scraps of fabrics are hand-sewn and stuffed to make this grand and glorious cape. Jessica Dvorak, the designer from Eugene, Ore., says, "Usually I wear whatever falls my way and only buy clothes at the Salvation Army. Just occasionally I get a craving for something special and have to design and make it myself."*

C-12. *Strips of bright, clear, cotton fabrics were sewn to the dress parts before the dress was assembled. The running stitch is a simple method of appliqué. By Jean Ray Laury.*

C-13. *Stacked layers of hand-stitched felt form the design on this felt skirt and vest. The cut at the lower edge of the vest repeats the shape of the felt appliqué. By Jean Ray Laury.*

C-14. *Bright-cotton appliqué on a dress by the imaginative and prolific designer, Jo Diggs.*

C-15. *"Rainbow Vest." Of Mexican handwoven cotton in layered appliqué. By Jo Diggs.*

C-16. *A simple velveteen cape, cut without a pattern, is lined with appliqué cottons. By Jean Ray Laury.*

C-17. *"Pelvic Plate." A fantasy costume of stuffed velvets with silk appliqué and beads. By Sas Colby, Ridgefield, Conn.*

C-18. *Yvonne Porcella, Modesto, Calif. combines dozens of pieces of fabric to create new patterns in her patchwork dresses. The mola, from the San Blas Islands, adds to an already special dress.*

C-19. *A floor-length sleeveless vest, or dress, uses plain and printed cottons for the hand appliqué of the large flowers. Cathy Lauridsen of San Francisco considers herself a fabric designer, and clothing offers a means of utilizing the fabrics she has designed.*

C-20. *Jo Diggs designed this skirt for Jenny Masterson, a superb potter who embellishes much of her work with horses. Jenny drew the horses, and Jo incorporated them into the hand-stitched cotton appliqué.*

C-21. *A simple long dress, worn by designer Yvonne Porcella, is enhanced by woven bands of brilliant color in a bib neck piece.*

C-22. *Back and front pieces of this silk cape are cut and batik-dyed before being joined at the shoulder seams. Red-orange and olive-green Procion dye combine for the three-color look. By Joyce Aiken, Clovis, Calif.*

11

12

13

15

16

17

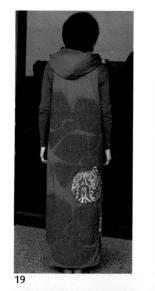

19

20

21

22

1-17. *Paisley shapes of solid embroidery embellish the entire surface of this vest. Designed, sewn, and worn by William Cahill Johnson, Canoga Park, Calif.*

1-18. *"Wedding Dress." To combine antique fabrics with new, Mr. Johnson first made a simple new dress of satin. An antique lace top was then drawn down over this to the waist and over the arms to partially cover the full sleeves. The lace added a sheer layer of detail and nostalgia. Around the bottom edge of the skirt he embroidered the California poppy and Illinois violet, flowers of the home states of the bride and groom, his son and daughter-in-law.*

1-19. Cross-stitch on blouse is accomplished by first stitching the cross-stitch canvas to the blouse. Then the stitching is done through both the canvas and the blouse fabric beneath it. When finished, the materials are dampened, and the canvas is drawn out, thread by thread. This leaves the stitching on the blouse. By June Moes, Woodland Hills, Calif.

these are the following: A dress cuff, resplendent in needlepoint, Figure C-82 (page 127); blouses with embroidery, Figures C-23 and 24, and the "Sun" in Figure C-28 (page 37), and variously embellished shirts and pants in Figures C-56, 59, and 67 (page 107).

FANCY PANTS

Embroidery for pants seems to have an appeal that is almost irresistible to anyone who plies a needle, but the greatest appeal is in blue denims. Few articles of clothing seem to intrigue people as much as denim clothes, jackets, or jeans. Perhaps it is the challenge of making the most out of the least or personalizing the biggest-selling mass-produced item of clothing. The seams of the garment tend to invite embroidery most of all. Few stitchers can resist elaborating on those double-sewn seams.

Sue Kensler's overalls show suns and flowers worked in embroidery floss, Figures 1-22 and 1-23. A stroll through any college campus, downtown, or in a ski or sun resort will reward you with a view of many hand-decorated jeans. Some are beautiful and complicated; many are simple and humorous. But all are personal, individual statements on an accepted, mass-produced pair of pants. In any part of the country young people, and a surprising number of older people, too, can be seen walking around with little sketches, doodles, or real works of art adorning their knees or posteriors. Some become human billboards, others are walking art galleries, and a few are the owners of telephone-booth doodle pants. Many of the examples shown here are not necessarily the best of what has been done. They are, rather, jeans which have been decorated by people with no experience, or background, in this work.

1-20

1-21

1-20. Cross-stitch on blouse by June Moes.

1-21. Detail of cross-stitch work in progress.

If you are a beginning embroiderer, you might do well to limit yourself (on a first project) to a portion of some clothing—cuffs, collar, yoke—or to an area on pants. After testing threads, yarns, skills, and materials, you will be ready to tackle a large job. Sue Kensler suggests that you avoid embroidery over the heavy seams in jeans, which are hard to sew through. Bea Slater compensates for that by using a pliers to pull the needle through these tight places. It is that tight fabric which must account for Liz Laury's saying, "I like to sew with my hands best, but sometimes I need my teeth and feet."

YARN EMBROIDERIES

Esther Feldman's beautiful yarn embroideries are incredibly rich and complex. As a stitchery teacher, she found herself with an assortment of weaving yarns, Persian wools, rug yarns, and hand-spuns of various textures and thicknesses. She also had an old army blanket with which she was unwilling, or unable, to part. The combination produced the blanket in Figure C-79 (page 110). The detail shown in Figure 1-36 gives a clear idea of the pattern of the stitches and how they are used. She cautions that you should consider the function of an object in selecting the stitches to be used. For example, on a sweater, long loops might catch and pull. When her use of stitches and textures is greatly varied, she limits the range of colors. She also reminds the would-be embroiderer that a sweater will be smaller in size after the knitted background is covered with layers of yarn. Keep tension loose, as knitting pulls out of shape with the

Text continues on p. 30

1-22

1-23

1-22. Few possessions are more highly prized by today's students than a nice worn pair of bib overalls—especially decorated as these are. They are a favorite of skiers, who find in bib overalls the comfort of a jump suit. By Sue Kensler, Eugene, Ore.

1-23. Another view of Sue Kensler's pants. She says, "Just the making of them is a blast. It's also fun to wear them."

1-24. Bea Slater's recycled blue jeans appear throughout this book, and she is shown here wearing a reclaimed denim jacket. The embroidery makes it very special, and she asks, "How else can I go to a social event without giving up my favorite clothes?"

1-25. "You Can't Get Good For Cheap." Embroidered pants combine quotations with flowers, suns, Mickey Mouse, hearts, snails, and whatever else struck the fancy of the stitcher. By Mary Becker, Woodland Hills, Calif.

1-26

1-28

1-27

1-26. Detail of outline and satin stitches in embroidery floss on denim pants. By Jean Ray Laury.

1-27. Embroidery on a stuffed form. By Esther Feldman.

1-28. A little romantic embroidery enriches the front of a dress. The design carries over from one side to the other when the dress front is buttoned. The pastoral scene is nestled between hills, which are suggested by the construction of the dress. By Phyllis Hall.

1-29

1-30

1-31

1-32

1-29. This delicately embroidered butterfly was found on a pair of pants at the Salvation Army.

1-30. A beautifully embroidered work shirt, using white and off-white yarns of various weights on faded blue. By Phyllis Hall.

1-31. "Love Grass." Cotton floss love-grass curls and tangles on the Levis, as it does on the ranch where the stitcher grew up. By Cam Smith, Los Angeles.

1-32. Patches and emblems are combined with embroidery on an Army fatigue jacket by Liz Laury.

1-33. Blue denim jacket by an anonymous artist.

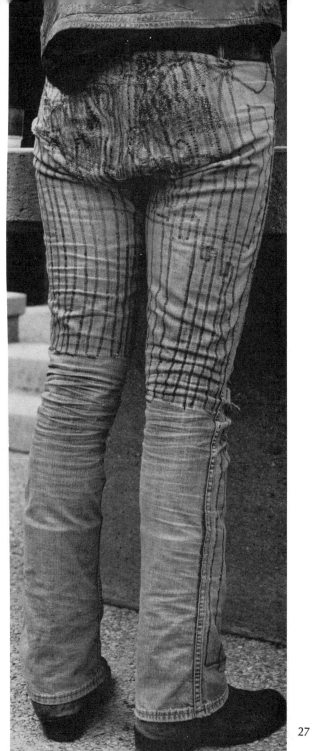

1-34. What started out as a way to patch a pair of worn pants grew into a way to decorate them. The operator of the sewing machine was obviously transported by the effect of her stitching! By Hetty Day, Fresno, Calif.

1-35. Esther Feldman's old sweater has become a lavish yarn embroidery, using stitches, non-loom weaving, and knotting.

1-36. An Army blanket, after being given survival therapy by Esther Feldman's needle. A great variety of yarns and stitches are combined in this beautifully designed piece.

1-35

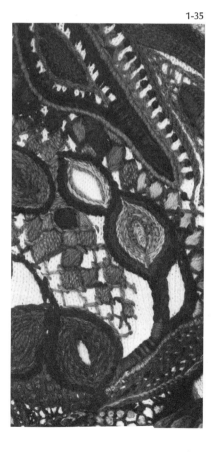

1-36

1-37. Knotting, braiding, embroidery, and stuffed velvets are part of an ever-continuing process on this cape. Dorothy Smaller, San Francisco, Calif., continues to sew on it as she wears it.

1-38. Needle-weaving, embroidery, appliqué, and beads are all used on this coat. What inspired Linda Witt to do the stitching was the fact that she didn't like the coat!

added weight of embroidery.

Charlotte Patera adds to this: "For embroidered clothing, don't cut final pattern piece until embroidery is finished. It may draw up. I always allow an extra inch around the edge to be cut off later." Charlotte enjoys the idea of embroidery on clothes, which allows her to express her own ideas in something unique that will not be duplicated. She feels that we are all tired of "mass production, being alike, following orders from Paris, etc. We are rebelling against status-symbol collecting."

Embroidery done by men is more common than many of us may have assumed. One good example is the work of William Cahill Johnson, whose vest in Figure 1-17 is solidly covered with yarn stitchery. Figure 1-18 shows more of his work.

FOR THE YOUNG SET

Esther Feldman's reworked, recycled, ecology-minded embroideries are greatly appreciated by young people. And she loves their patches, created and worn with joy. They remind her of Depression days when you patched creatively, but then sat (hiding the patches) while you paged through the magazines, looking at the latest Paris fashions!

Another woman whose ambitious embroidery knows no bounds is Linda Witt. Her coat, shown in Figure C-69 (page 110) is a composite of many fiber-working techniques. A detail is shown in Figure 1-38.

Stitching is among the most joyous of the decorative arts, and embroidery is at the heart of stitching. Hopefully, the examples in this book will inspire you if you are just beginning—or further enrich the range of possibilities if you are already an expert. These pages simply offer a means for people of all ages and talents to share the delight they find in fixing up their clothes!

2-1

2-1. Hearts, flowers and birds combine on a cape decorated by Norman Laliberté with permanent marking pen and dye paint.

2-2. Designs were drawn with permanent marking pens on ready-to-wear pants and shirt. Designer Aaron Bartell of Eugene, Ore., is interested in making a design "which both reshapes the body in the observer's eye and can stand alone as a three-dimensional art work."

2. Printed and Painted

Painting directly on fabric would seem to be an irresistible invitation to the person who feels at home with a paint brush. Rather than work on lengths of fabric, either the pattern parts or a completed garment can be decorated with paint. The painting merges with the body form. The silk-screening process or block printing offers the opportunity to design specifically for a dress, shirt, skirt, and so on, rather than to accept the common limitations of cutting garment parts from printed material.

New paints and dyes, made available in the last few years, have increased the interest in printing and painting fabrics. Many of these products can be used without special equipment or formulas. Only a minimum of space and paints, along with a desire to create a unique or unusual body covering, are necessary to start.

CHOICE OF FABRICS

Certain kinds of fabrics must be used if the paints and dyes are to remain permanent. Cotton, linen, silk and some rayons give you the best results, but they must be washed first. Do not use fabrics that have been specially treated for crease resistance or are permanent press as they will not take the dye easily.

Few clothes are more exuberantly decorated or softly colorful than those painted by K. Lee Manuel, Figures C-35 and 36 (page 56) and C-77 and 78 (page 110). Her world is full of fantasy and has been since she was a child. At one time she exhibited her textiles in galleries, but they soon came off the wall and

Text continues on p. 40

2-3

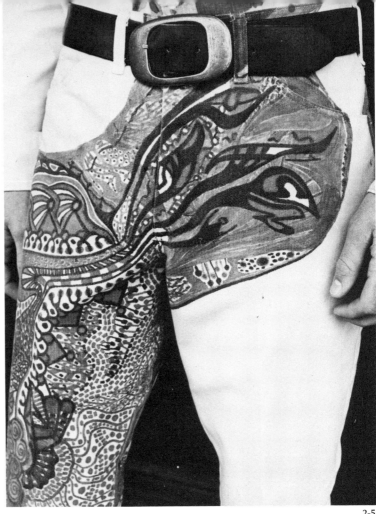

2-4

2-5

2-3 and 4. Third-grade students in a Los Angeles classroom made simple, brilliant-colored designs on squares of muslin. Their teacher set the marking-pen drawings by dipping them in a salt solution and pressing with a hot iron. The blocks were stitched together, making the movable gallery into a skirt for the teacher.

2-5. Detail of Figure 2-2.

2-6

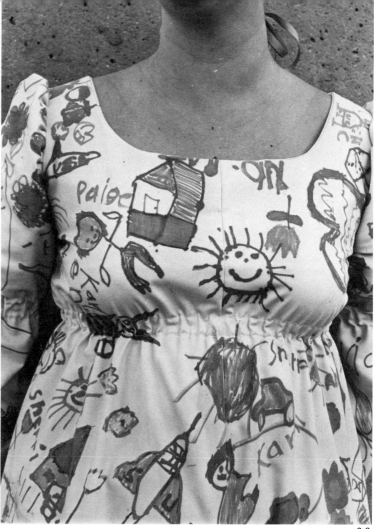

2-7

2-8

2-6. *Kindergarten teacher Margaret Miller, Fresno, Calif., made a pants suit from fabric on which her students had made delightful and colorful drawings with permanent marking pens.*

2-7. *A baseball shirt was stretched and tacked over a piece of cardboard to keep it taut. Marking pen could then move easily over the knit fabric to make the design. By Joyce Aiken.*

2-8. *Detail of pants suit by Margaret Miller. The decorating project was planned so that Margaret could wear the children's drawings to Parents' Night Open House at her school.*

2-9

2-10

2-11

2-9. An embroidered rice sack has had its printed side appliquéd to the back of a ready-made shirt. By Jean Ray Laury.

2-10. A horse-feed sack is used to make a shirt which an avid horse-lover finds great fun to wear. This one gets added attention when the letters are outlined with marking pen. By Jean Ray Laury.

2-11. A printed pink satin souvenir pillow top has finally found a home on the back of a shirt, making the best use of the worst that was available. It was beaded and padded before being attached with an edging of glass beads. By Joyce Aiken.

2-12

2-13

2-14

2-12. Borders of two skirts are silk-screen printed by designer Becky Biller of Ventura, Calif. The simple cut of each dress allows the print design to keep its importance.

2-13 and 14. Details of silk-screened dresses, Figure 2-12.

C-23. Shells, attached at the waist, add movement to a velvet shirt using beads, appliqué, and embroidery. Made and worn by Gabriella McMillen, Topanga, Calif.

C-24. Delicate embroidery of provincial design borders the front opening and the cuffs of this blouse. The center of each button is also embroidered. By Charlotte Patera, Mill Valley, Calif.

C-25. Bright yarns frame and hold tiny mirrors in place on a dress top, designed and worn by Jean Simpson, Glendale, Calif. The mirrors sparkle and reflect with each movement of the body so that the garment takes on life when it is worn.

C-26. "Tulip Shirt." A plain cotton shirt becomes elegant with the chain-stitched embroidery of designer and model Bets Barnard, San Diego, Calif.

C-27. "Regal Rice Shirt." The design of a printed rice bag is accentuated with embroidery. Outline stitches and running stitches edge the boundaries of the letters. Satin stitches cover the rice images. The entire printed area of the bag was appliquéd to the shirt first. In this way, the embroidery stitches hold the layers securely together. By Jean Ray Laury.

C-28. The meticulously worked embroidery of this vest incorporates intricate signs and symbols of special importance to the wearer. By Susan Atkins, Frontera, Calif.

C-29. Tie-and-dye, using discharge process on cotton undershirt. By Joyce Aiken.

C-30. The rich texture of cotton velvet is brilliantly tie-dyed and beaded in this striking dress by Masako Takahashi, Los Angeles, Calif.

C-31 and 32. Leather "Body Bags" by Yvonne Porcella. They are enhanced by wool yarn, woven, wrapped, and fringed. She has designed them to be transferred from shoulder to wall when not in use.

C-33. Undershirts, T-shirts, and baseball shirts are easy projects for tie-dye. By Joyce Aiken.

C-34. An insect, embedded in a prehistoric stone, inspired the design for this batik skirt. By Baroness Jessie Von Fersen.

23

24

25

26

27

28

29

30

31

32

33

34

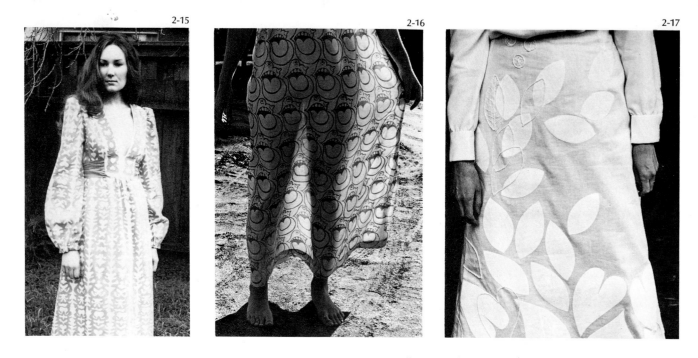

2-15. Silk-screened dress by Jeanette Melnick of Cleveland, Ohio, makes use of the negative (unprinted) shapes as part of the design.

2-16. Silk-screen print, in a repeat design, covered the silk fabric before it was cut into a simple dress. By Cay Lang, Sanger, Calif.

2-17. A leaf design is silk-screened on a thin white fabric with white opaque ink. Embroidery and couching with white threads and yarns embellish the surface. By Joyce Aiken.

2-18

2-18. Acrylic paint brightens up and gives new life to a pair of pants by Doug Hansen. The shirt has a satin star padded and appliquéd to it.

2-19 and 21. Morality messages are printed on sweat shirts by silk-screen printing. By Ruth Law and Jean Ray Laury.

2-20. Cotton velveteen is an excellent fabric for silk-screen prints. Judy Calandra, Fresno, Calif., printed this velveteen in two colors.

2-22. The design for this shirt is cut from stencil paper and taped to the shirt with double-stick tape. A sheet of newspaper goes inside the shirt for protection, and the design is spray-painted with fabric paint. By Jackie Vermeer, Concord, Calif.

2-19

2-20

2-21

2-22

39

holes were cut in the centers so they could be worn. She designs one-of-a-kind body coverings because she is dissatisfied with the concept of clothes in our society as merely fashion. It is her hope that her creations will help evolve a new consciousness about the body becoming a dynamic part of everyday space.

K. Lee cuts her clothes from muslin and decorates them with the water-soluble textile paint Versatex. Stiff bristle brushes work better for applying the paint than soft brushes. After the paint is completely dry, the fabric pieces are put into a clothes dryer for 40 minutes to set the color. Some sections of a design are padded before sewing fabric parts together. Brightly colored feathers and fringes add to the fantasy outfits. Her "Indian Princess" dress, Figure 2-27, shows a strong geometric pattern in golds, blues and browns.

THE MARKING PEN

Every child who has taken a marking pen to his knee, shirt sleeve or paper will love decorating his own clothes. An even more delightful solution is seen in Margaret Miller's wildly joyous pants suit, Figure 2-8. She cut the fabric parts, sewed up the front seam, and then turned her kindergarten students loose with their pens. Each drew a picture for her and signed his name. What a great way to remember a class of students in later years!

The outfit in Figure 2-2 shows the use of marking pens in making a three-dimensional drawing-painting over the body. Starting with ready-made pants and shirt, the designer let his drawing wrap and flow around the body. Figure 2-5 shows the extent to which a marking pen can be used for small and intricate detail.

A hooded cape is brightly decorated with the familiar drawings of designer Norman Laliberté, Figure 2-1 and C-5 (frontispiece). The marking pen outlines, dots and fills in areas of the design with colorful abandon.

PRE-PRINTED MATERIALS

Ready-printed materials (sugar sacks, burlap bags or advertising banners) offer a good beginning for working on printed fabrics. Feed sacks are probably the most readily available. In Figure 2-10 a pre-printed grain sack is made into a shirt with the lettering outlined by marking pen.

Some fabrics accept the inks better than others, though a marking pen is one of the few dyes that works well on permanent-press fabrics. You should experiment with pens and fabrics before launching on a large project. Iron the fabric when finished to help set the color, and always work in a well-ventilated room, as the fumes from the pen bother some people.

The "Regal Rice Shirt," Figure 2-9 makes use of the printed side of a rice bag. A section of the bag is appliquéd to the back of a ready-made shirt with running stitch around the edges. Some of the letters are outlined with running stitches, others with outline stitches. The rice is covered solidly with satin stitches.

It is not always necessary to have the best to work with. At times, even the worst can be an inspiration. A satin souvenir pillow from San Francisco is trite enough to be great, and is here added to a satin bowling shirt for a truly funky garment, Figure 2-11. The printed and fringed pillow top was treated with beads, embroidery and padding.

2-23 and 24. Joyce Aiken looks at you from the front and back of sweat shirts she silk-screened for her family. A photograph is enlarged, put on photo-sensitive film, and adhered to a silk screen for printing.

SILK-SCREEN PRINTING

Silk-screen printing offers an opportunity for multiple-image designing, whether it be a repeat design on fabric, or one image printed on many garments. A repeated design takes on different forms as the unit creates new shapes in juxtaposition, as in Figure 2-20. The print for the dress in Figure 2-15 was silk-screened onto a length of material before the material was cut into pattern parts. Designing the print to fit cut pattern shapes is also possible. The butterfly on the bottom of the skirt in Figure 2-14 fills the width of the fabric piece and is printed as a single unit. That part of the pattern design would not need to change for the dress to fit any size wearer.

Oil-base inks, used for silk-screen printing on paper, can be used on fabric although it stiffens the material where it is applied. The sweatshirts in Figures 2-19 and 21 are printed with this ink, as is the skirt in Figure 2-17. After many washings, the ink will become less intense in color. The shirts in Figure 2-23 are also printed with oil-base ink. Designer Joyce Aiken used a photo silk-screen method for printing her own image on sweatshirts for her family.

Screen- and block-printing also allow for the design of forms and colors that grow out of the body shape. For example, collars, necklaces, jewelry, or arm bands can be printed directly onto shirt parts, or onto a finished shirt. One printer, in jest, screened buttons, buttonholes, and zippers over a shirt front. The printing need not always suggest the additional cover or layers. It is sometimes used to reveal. A silk-screen photo-print of her own nude figure was screened front and back on pants and shirt by a design student.

The equipment needed for silk-screen printing includes a frame stretched with silk, a squeegee, block-out (lacquer film), dye and a padded table for printing. Art stores and special silk-screen suppliers

2-25. Detail of "White Feather Neckpiece" shows the character of the dye-painted and drawn lines on velveteen.

2-26. "White Feather Neckpiece" is a sculptured form by Lenore Davis. Stuffed gloves wrap around the body and fingers, or feathers of cotton velveteen, painted with Procion dye, form a fringe pattern around the shoulders.

handle the inks, dyes and equipment for printing. It may seem difficult to cut and adhere the lacquer film at first, but a little practice gives you confidence. Water-soluble Procion dye or Inko dye produce permanent color after being set by heat. They can be used for silk-screening or for direct painting.

PAINTED FABRIC

The velveteen feather neckpiece in Figure 2-26 has been stuffed with polyester and painted with Procion dye. Lenore Davis works primarily in soft sculpture, and she brings that direction and approach to her clothing design. She regards clothes as sculptural forms, and considers them to be joyful and personal pieces on which to work. She cuts her fabric pieces carefully, with concern for the nap of the fabric. Color deepens on nap going up and lightens on nap coming down. The dye can be applied to the fabric with a paint brush, plastic squeeze bottles, tjantings, paint rollers, sponges or whatever will hold the ink from dye container to fabric. See Figures C-41 (page 90) and C-91 (page 127) for other examples of Lenore Davis's painted and padded body coverings.

Acrylic paint is a quick and easy medium to use for decorating cloth. The pants in Figure 2-18 have been treated to stars and stripes with acrylics. The paint remains flexible so there is no problem with it crackling when the fabrics fold.

2-27

2-28

2-27. Indian Princess dress by K. Lee Manuel is decorated with textile paint. Buckskin thongs, strung with beads, lace up the front.

2-28. The beauty of a seashell is captured in paint on this shirt by K. Lee Manuel. It is padded and stitched to give a quilted effect.

⊚. Fibers

Working with threads and yarns is a natural and basic approach to body coverings and one well known to silkworms and tent caterpillars! Weaving is the oldest of the fiber techniques. Macramé and free crochet are the latest to re-emerge as popular clothing crafts. No matter what method is used for putting fibers together, it is a flexible medium. Macramé cords can spread apart or close up to fit the figure. Crochet can be sculptural as well as functional.

MACRAMÉ

Macramé pieces are often used as embellishments for other garments. They become texture and linear patterns over plain or smooth fabrics. The loose cords, left hanging and untied, swirl around the body to create a moving contour as seen in Figure 3-7. The pattern includes just the most basic of macramé knots, and those even the beginner can easily learn. These are the half hitch and square knots. The vest in Figure 3-3 is worked with half hitches using eight shades of orange yarn. Leather conchettas are attached on the front and back.

Cotton seine cord is popular for macramé garments. It can be left natural or dyed a color as in the vest in Figure 3-4. The cord is cut to the correct length and dyed before knotting. When dying cord, wash first to remove filler or surface coating so the dye takes evenly. Macramés in Figures 3-1 and 6 use the natural, undyed seine cord so that the square knot pattern can easily be seen. Text continues on p. 49

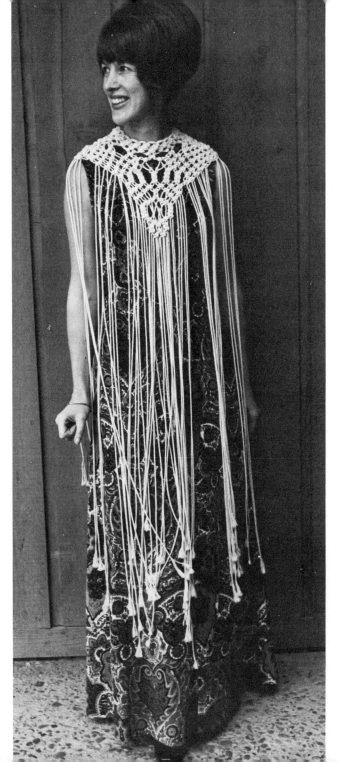

3-1. Macramé collar becomes an elegant cape when cords fall from the neck to the floor. By Jack Dunstan, Saratoga, Calif.

3-2

3-3

3-2. A crochet vest develops freely within the framework of a paper pattern. By Sue Donleavey, Clovis, Calif.

3-3. Vest by Everett K. Sturgeon, Oakdale, Pa. The texture of macramé knots combines with smooth leather.

3-4. A pullover macramé vest by Jack Dunstan was worked over a dress form.

3-5. Gold cord is used by Louise Murphy, Fresno, Calif., in her macramé collar with cords dropping almost to the floor.

3-6. An over-garment by Jack Dunstan is made with macramé, using #36 cotton seine cord.

3-4

3-5

3-6

3-7. Nylon seine twine is dyed and macramé-knotted into a garment by Linda Allen, La Verne, Calif. She uses a mannequin to hold the twine in place while knotting.

3-8. Heavy crochet edging was made for the hem, sleeves, and neckline to contrast with the simple lines of a dress. By Joanne Derr.

3-10

3-9. Flowers provide windows to let bare skin show between strands of the Swedish linen yarns used for the crochet. By Christina Luell, Los Angeles, Calif.

3-10. Detail of crochet dress by Christina Luell shows the contrast of flower shapes to regular crochet stitches.

3-9

3-11. Bonnie Meltzer began making neck pieces as wearable paintings/tapestries. Her "Bib with Face" is crochet, and the edging is upholstery fringe.

Macramé designing is easy to control when knotting is worked on a fabric dress form. Start with a holding cord at the neckline. Attach other cords to it and begin the pattern. It is possible to work the whole pattern without the addition of new cords, as it is easy to open and close the shape.

CROCHET

The technique of crochet allows the adding and decreasing of stitches with such ease that it is an ideal medium for enclosing the body. A few years ago crochet found its way into art galleries in the form of sculpture. By adapting some of the techniques used in soft sculpture, designers can crochet much more exciting clothes than when using traditional designs.

Figure 3-2 shows the start of a free-crochet vest that will follow a paper pattern for fit. This allows the designer freedom to create within a planned framework. For some artists, body coverings are an extension of their gallery work. Bonnie Meltzer's "Bib with Face" in Figure 3-11 is a wearable tapestry. She uses different brands and kinds of yarn in one piece to achieve a richness of texture and color.

Phyllis Neufeld is another artist who has taken her craft off the wall and put it on to the body. Her full-length crochet dress is elegant in its color and texture Figure C-44 (page 90).

OFF-THE-LOOM WEAVING

Off-the-loom weaving gives the beginner a chance to experiment with yarns. The vest in Figure 3-15 is woven on a piece of heavy cardboard. A pattern is cut in cardboard to the proper size and shape. Slits are made on opposite ends and warp thread attached. The weaving follows the shape of the pattern. When finished, the woven piece is removed from the cardboard. After all parts are woven, they are joined together to make the vest.

Text continues on p. 52

3-12

3-13

3-14

3-16

3-12. Wrapped yarns make a stand-up collar for a card-woven vest by Candace Crockett, Woodside, Calif,

3-13. Detail of neck piece.

3-14. Karakul sheep fleece makes a fringe that adds elegance to a card-woven neck piece by Candace Crockett.

3-15. Woven vest by Phylliss Hall uses cardboard pattern shapes with slits in the ends to hold warp threads. The weaving follows the cardboard shape and, when removed, is joined to other woven pieces worked the same way.

3-16. A simple and beautiful card-woven scarf uses weft threads for fringe. By Candace Crockett.

CARD WEAVING

Card-woven strips can be sewn together to make clothes with interesting and intricate designs. Figure 3-12 shows a card-woven cape with wrapped stand-up collar. The strips join and weave together to achieve the form. The fringe on the neck piece in Figure 3-14 occurs when a new length of sheep's fleece, used as the weft, is added on alternate rows. The extra length becomes the fringe. See detail of collar, Figure 3-13. A similar treatment of wool fringe is used on the scarf in Figure 3-16.

LOOM WEAVING

Traditional loom weaving takes on added interest when it covers the three-dimensional form of the body. Fringes, feathers and unspun wool all add texture to the otherwise plain surface of the woven cloth. A shirt woven by John Garret makes use of colored yarns, fringe and loops in bands to create a surface full of texture, Figure 3-21.

Barbara Setsu Pickett designs ceremonial body coverings for use in mythical rites. She believes that "Ceremonial textiles are vehicles for transporting us from the mundane, habitual, utilitarian, and ordinary into the realm of the unexpected and extraordinary." Her "Cloak for Endymion," Figure 3-25, is made of mohair and white wool roving wrapped with linen yarn and sewn on a handwoven, weft-faced wool cloth. The tapestry moon uses the same material. The circular cape in Figure 3-27 is worn with a snake helmet. The snakes are wrapped elements of jute cord covered with rayon rug yarn and sewn on to both the cape and the helmet.

Many designers express a feeling about body cov-

Text continues on p. 60

3-17. A card-woven band holds wrapped fringe that drops from the shoulders of this cape by Jack Dunstan.

3-18

3-19

3-20

3-21

3-18. Strips of card weaving are sewn together to make a vest by Diana Mitchell, San Jose, Calif. Warp threads form the fringe.

3-19. Card-woven strips made with natural hand-spun fleece join together to make this purse. By Candace Crockett.

3-20. "Belt with Tassels" uses goat hair in the weaving, fringe, and tassels. By Candace Crockett.

3-21. Bands of color combine with loops and fringe in a shirt woven and modeled by John Garret, Claremont, Calif.

3-22

3-24

3-22 and 23. "Helmets." Jute cord is wrapped with hand-spun, natural-dyed wool yarn and then coiled. Feathers add texture and color to the helmets that practically encase the head. By Barbara Setsu Pickett, Portland, Ore.

3-24. Woven strips combine with wrapped and fringed yarns to cover this leather body bag by Yvonne Porcella.

3-23

3-25. "Cloak for Endymion." An elegant white-on-white cloak with mohair and wool roving, sewn onto a handwoven cloth. A tapestry moon adds delicacy. By Barbara Setsu Pickett.

3-26. "Winter Ceremonial Cape." Brown alpaca roving is wrapped with gray hair and heather-toned wool; then sewn onto gray wool cloth. The yoke hook is brown suede. By Barbara Setsu Pickett.

35

36

37

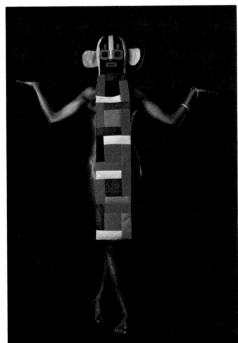

38

39

C-35. The talented and imaginative K. Lee Manuel of San Francisco paints exuberant designs and color on cotton fabrics. Here she has bedecked all the kids in the neighborhood. K. Lee is the person peering at the camera.

C-36. Textile paint, when handled by K. Lee Manuel, transforms inexpensive muslin into a mobile painting. The shirt is formed of squares and rectangles. Feathered cords are used as laces under the arms.

C-37. "Cape." Body movement turns this cape into kinetic sculpture, as every turn of the body puts tassels and tails in motion. By Sas Colby.

C-38. "Elephant Mask." A fantasy mask of patchwork with body bib. By Sas Colby.

C-39. "Patchwork Cape." Imaginative use of a traditional quilt-block design adds optical illusion to a brilliant pattern. By Sas Colby.

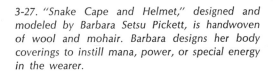

3-27. "Snake Cape and Helmet," designed and modeled by Barbara Setsu Pickett, is handwoven of wool and mohair. Barbara designs her body coverings to instill mana, power, or special energy in the wearer.

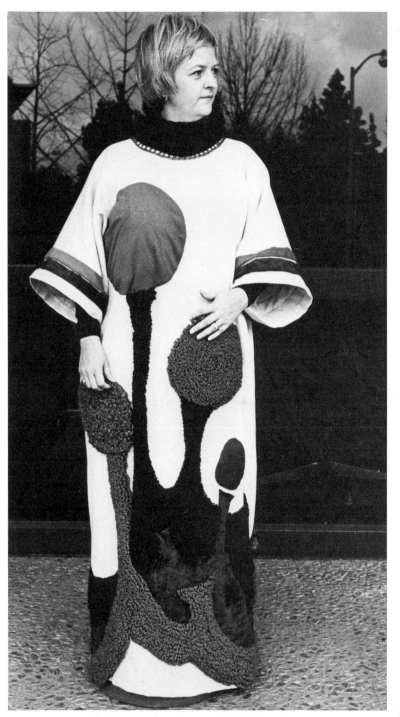

3-28. Appliqué of felt and velvet combines with hooked yarns to make the trees grow from the hem of this dress. By Jerrie Peters, Fresno, Calif.

3-29

3-29. A handwoven stole is fringed with cords that are wrapped, braided, and then wrapped again. By Dorothy Smaller.

3-30. Crochet vest, by Toni Horgos of San Francisco, Calif., combines leather with natural and dyed yarns.

3-31. A hole punch was used to perforate the cut pieces of leather. Yarns were then attached by crocheting through the holes in a heavy, handsome vest. By Toni Horgos.

3-32. Detail of Figure 3-31.

erings similar to that of Barbara Setsu Pickett. Their clothes give the wearer special or magical power, or take him out of his everyday existence, lifting him to a plateau. There is a personal involvement with the creation of a piece of cloth to be worn by another individual that differs from the production of a wall hanging. The fiber craftsman especially feels this as he carefully selects each piece of thread and yarn that goes into his body covering.

3-32

3-30

3-31

3-33. Hundreds of short lengths of hand-spun wool yarn samples were crocheted into this extravagant cape by Maggie Brosnan of San Jose, Calif. The tubular and stringlike dangles are yarn, wrapped wood spools, keys, beads, and dye labels.

4. Appliqué

The fastest, easiest way to personalize and add brilliant color to clothing is with appliqué. It means simply to apply one piece of cut fabric to another. There are many ways of doing this, but among the easiest of all is felt appliqué.

FELT

Felt is non-woven, and, therefore, it does not ravel. Edges need not be turned under or finished. The material itself offers so little resistance that the needle slips through it easily. It is a remarkably easy material to use, so if it is not the most durable one, that is at least compensated for by the speed with which it can be sewn.

Felt clothes require dry cleaning, though small pieces of felt on other fabrics can be laundered. As felts are usually wool and rayon, they shrink in washing or under a steam iron.

Several photographs of felt clothing are shown in Figures C-1, 13, and 76. (Frontispiece and pages 19 and 110. Each uses the very simplest of all sewing techniques—the running stitch. Because of the thickness and softness of felt, the stitches make a nice pattern at the sewn edges.

The garments themselves are very simple, with few seams. See Drawing 1. Edges can be left raw or they can be bound. Figure C-46 shows a band of

Text continues on p. 66

4-1. A skiing cape is bright red, appliquéd with a fringe of panels at the hem. Slits at the front allow for arm movement. By Jean Ray Laury.

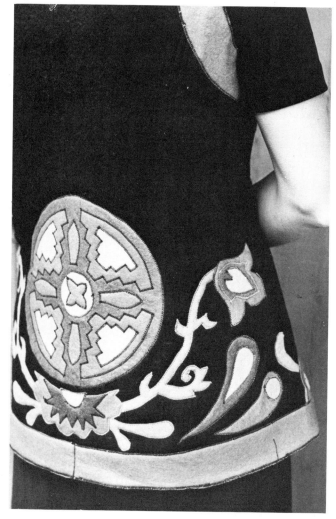

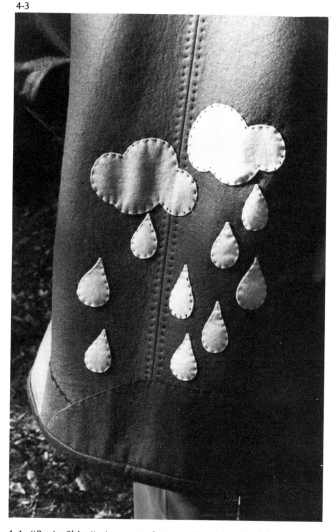

4-2. "Vest." Brightly colored felts are appliquéd with machine stitching to a black felt vest. A narrow zigzag stitch adds a line of color at each edge. By Harlene Anthony.

4-3. "Rainbow Shirt." This pullover is cut from felt in simple, large shapes. It is then appliquéd with more felt. A running stitch, using a single strand of mercerized thread, gives a pattern or texture to the edge of the appliquéd pieces. The amount of pattern, or pucker, can be controlled by the tautness of the sewing threads. By Jean Ray Laury.

4-4. "Bea's Shirt." A sweat shirt, appliquéd with felt cutouts, and sewn with running stitch. If appliqué is done on a new (unwashed) sweat shirt, both materials will shrink in washing and will still fit one another. Turn the garment inside out during washing. If you appliqué felt to an old sweat shirt, allow extra fullness in the felt, or preshrink the felt by dipping in warm water. This shirt was appliquéd for Bea Slater by Jean Ray Laury.

4-5. "Heart." An overcast stitch holds the felt firmly in place on the sweat shirt. Use a thread that matches the color of the piece you are appliquéing. By Jean Ray Laury.

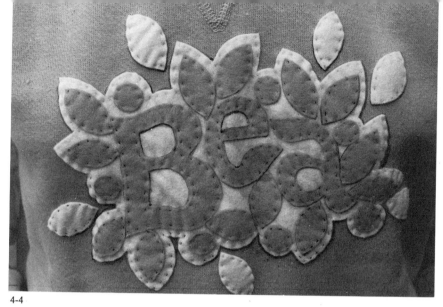

4-4

4-5

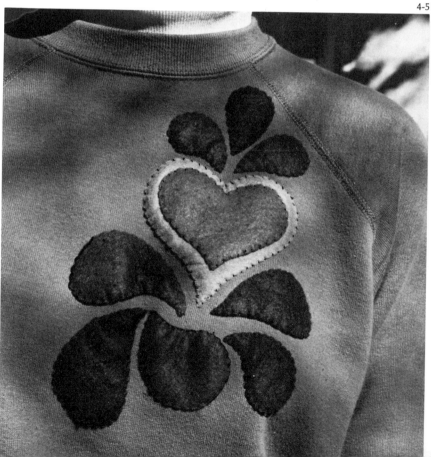

Drawing 1. Very simple cuts are best for felt garments. You can cut your own patterns by using a shirt or pullover which is the correct size for you. Cut around the shirt, using neckline and sleeves as guides. Allow extra material for seams, and make felt garments full, since the material is heavy.

4-6. "Ribbon Dress." Bands of laces and edgings almost cover the original fabric of this dress by Janice Rosenberg, Fresno, Calif.

4-7. Detail of ribbons and edgings on skirt.

felt used for finishing the cut edge. Complex patterns, gathering, set-in sleeves, collars and small cut pieces are not appropriate for felt, as the material becomes too bulky.

Barbara Kensler's felt dress, Figure C-50 (page 90), incorporates the decorative appliqué with the binding. She uses a whip stitch, or an overcast stitch, in applying the cut shapes. This gives an interesting edge, and it is a fast, simple stitch to do. French knots are added in a wool yarn.

A running stitch is used for the appliqués in Figures 4-3 and 4. The overcast stitch, which is used in Figure 4-5, gives a different pattern to the material. These stitches are shown in Drawings 2 and 3.

Machine stitching can also be used on felt, either a zigzag or satin stitch, or a straight stitch. The vest in Figure 4-2 is a great example of a beautifully finished machine appliqué.

IRON-ON TAPE

The only appliqué method easier than felt is that of iron-on tape. Because the tape comes in strips, or patch-sized pieces, designs must be cut to fit within

4-6

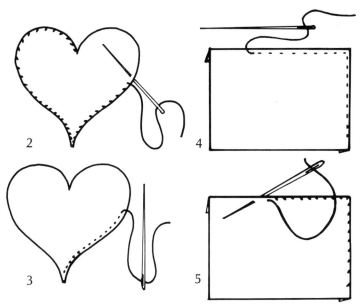

2

3

4

5

Drawings 2 and 3. Felt can be appliquéd without turning under the edges. Either an overcast stitch (2), or a running stitch (3), is suitable.

Drawings 4 and 5. To appliqué woven materials by hand, turn under about ¼" of the fabric. Keep stitches very near the folded edge in the running stitch (3). An overcast stitch (5) looks best if the needle dips under the fold of the fabric in starting each new stitch. This makes a firm stitch and adds fullness to the shape being appliquéd.

that size limitation. The backing material should be able to withstand the hot iron which attaches the iron-on tape to the fabric. Figures 4-9 and 10 show a batiste dress decorated in this way. If you use iron-on tape for a garment that is washed frequently, a line of machine stitching at the edge will give additional strength and prevent eventual fraying.

HAND-SEWN APPLIQUÉ

Hand-sewn appliqué is more durable than most people assume. It can withstand machine washing if an ample amount of fabric edge has been turned under. Either a running stitch, an overcast, or a blind stitch can be used. Turn under the edges of the material as you sew. See Drawings 4 and 5.

Jody House has incorporated her cut-through appliqués in a jumper in Figure 4-8. The individual panels are appliquéd to the skirt, while the bib section is a separate appliqué. Details, Figure C-65 and 66 (page 107), show blind-stitch appliqués.

RIBBONS AND BINDINGS

Another simplified approach to appliqué is to use ribbons, edgings, or bindings. As these have pre-finished edges, nothing need be turned under. It is easiest to work by cutting the fabric pieces out first so that you have, for example, a sleeve laid flat. Sew all ribbons, edgings, or appliqué strips to the sleeve *before* joining the garment parts. Appliqués can be cut and added afterwards. Figure 4-6 shows a dress frosted with laces and edgings appliquéd over a solid material.

The shirts in Figures C-2 and 4 (frontispiece) are covered with ribbons, edgings, and bindings, all attached with a straight machine stitch. Two or three colors of yardage may be sewn together and the pattern parts cut out. Some color changes then occur before the addition of ribbons. Again, all ribbons, or edgings, are sewn to the flat parts of the shirt before it is assembled.

STUFFING AND PADDING

Stuffing and padding grow easily from appliqué. Jessica Dvorak's stuffed cape in Figure C-11 (page 19) is a gorgeous example of appliqués filled with padding. In a more precise use of padding, Marilyn Stern

Text continues on p. 78

4-8. "Jumper." Cut-through appliqué is worked in squares, which are then sewn to a band on the bottom of the skirt. These add a rich relief pattern to contrast with the smooth areas of solid color. Cut-through appliqué, in which layers of materials are stacked and the design is cut from the top, is more difficult to manage than regular appliqué. It would not be the best project for someone trying appliqué for the first time. By Jody House.

4-9. "Humming Birds." Flower forms cut from iron-on tape transform this simple white dress. The pattern of iron-on tape flowers encircles each sleeve and the hemline. By Jean Ray Laury.

4-10. Detail of "Humming Birds." As pieces are cut, they are ironed in place. The dress fabric is cotton batiste; the tape, cotton. Iron-on patches for blue jeans are of much heavier fabric and should be reserved for use on heavier materials.

4-11. Shirt, using crocheted baubles from a thrift-store handbag. The weighted pendants of crochet move and turn with the wearer. The crochet is in off-white on a homespun pullover. By Joyce Aiken.

4-12. Ribbons and doilies combine with edgings and appliqué in this gold, yellow, and white shirt by Jean Ray Laury.

4-13. "Vestment," made from cotton velveteen, is appliquéd with velveteens and cottons. The lining is bright taffeta. Appliqués are done with a blind stitch and are most easily sewn while the pieces of the vestment are still flat. By Jean Ray Laury. (See also Figure C-51, page 90.)

4-14. Cotton T-shirts are appliquéd with pieces of nylon tricot, then stuffed from underneath. Hand or machine stitching then provides a quilted effect. By Marilyn Stern, Portland, Ore.

4-15. Detail of one of Marilyn Stern's T-shirts, showing the padding.

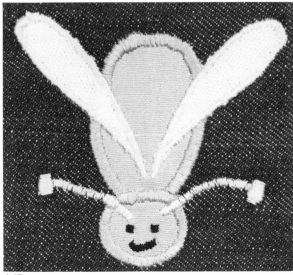

4-16. Detail showing back of "Vest with Medals." By Sas Colby.

4-17 and 19. Patches for jeans, drawn by Tamelin McNutt, and sewn by her mother.

4-18. "Vest with Medals." Real medals combine with ribbons, appliqué, and fringes in a vest designed to make a hero of every man. By Sas Colby.

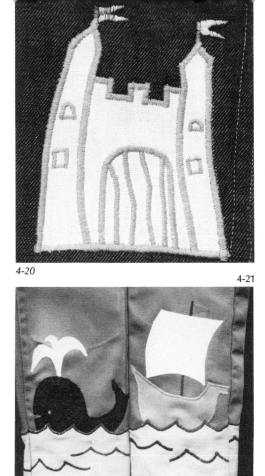

4-20

4-21

4-22

4-20. "Castle." The drawings of Cass McNutt were used by his mother to add designs over the knees of worn jeans. A dragon covers the other knee of Cass's favorite pants.

4-21. "High-Water Pants." To lengthen outgrown pants, a band is cut from the bottom of another outgrown pair. These are machine-sewn with a satin stitch to suggest high-water. The ship and whale are imaginative and decorative additions to delight any child. By Gloria McNutt.

4-22. Dress shows how the design of the fabric may inspire ideas and possibilities for appliqué. Here, the fabric used for the bodice is repeated in color through the checkered material of the sleeves and in design through the appliqué. The small flowers in the bodice fabric are enlarged and cut from cotton fabrics; then appliquéd to the skirt with a blind stitch. By Joyce Aiken.

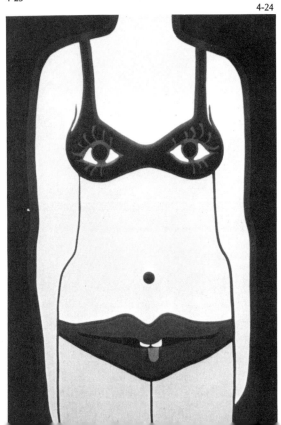

4-23. Apron in white-on-white muslin uses appliqué and running stitch. By Priscilla Beeching, Fresno, Calif.

4-24. "Bikini Baby." The headless body in this stitchery panel is Jo Diggs' statement about body culture. Though it is not actually a garment, she uses the garment as a means of making a personal social comment.

4-25. Burlap provides a strong-textured background for smooth satins and cottons in a colorful lined vest. By Pat Mace, Santa Monica, Calif.

4-27. "Snake Cape." A long cape, lined in yellow satin, has a serpent which crawls and curls the full length of the cape. The head and tail wrap around so that when the cape is closed the head and tail of the snake come to the outside. By Jean Ray Laury.

26. "Magic Cape." Various fabrics are used in the appliqué magic symbols to the heavy cape, which also incorporates broidery for details. By Christalene, Topanga, Calif.

75

4-28

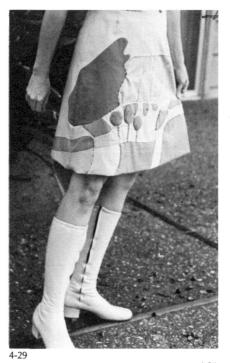

4-29

4-30

4-28. Fabric appliqué is done in a block-on-block pattern. The large shape is sewn to the sweat shirt last. By Joyce Aiken.

4-29. Joan Schulze of Sunnyvale, Calif., sewed this cut-through and appliquéd skirt of cottons and suede cloth.

4-30. Drawings by Cyndi (4½) and Scott (7) are transferred from paper to fabric: they are used to decorate a dress and hat for Cyndi, sewn by their mother, Kathy Miller, Fresno. A zigzag machine stitch was used to appliqué the cut shapes. Black crochet thread was used for embroidery details.

4-31. Appliquéd clouds and sunshine make these blue jeans very special to this boy. By Simone Gad.

4-32. Machine appliqué adds colorful exotic birds to a little girl's dress. The designer, Mimi Shimmin, recommends attaching iron-on interfacing to the back side of the cotton fabric before cutting out the appliqués. The added stiffness makes the machine appliqué easier to handle.

4-31

4-32

4-34

4-33

4-33. Snow pullover, in wool with felt appliqué, adds warmth and color for a tobogganer. Hand appliquéd by Marilyn Judson, Davis, Calif.

4-34. Detail of appliqué. Buttons and loops on a dress by Gloria McNutt. The full dress is shown in Figure C-75 (page 110).

4-35. "Rainbow Vest." Detail from another of Jo Digg's masterly hand-sewn stitchery garments.

4-35

4-36

4-37

4-36. Jenny Masterson's skirt is a richly appliquéd fabric by Jo Diggs. The full skirt is shown in Figure C-20 (page 19).

4-37. A suit coat, with colored appliqué on the lapels, is ready to transfer from office to party! The necktie has a stuffed stocking-face doll appliquéd to it. Coat by Joyce Aiken; tie by Jean Ray Laury.

has appliquéd nylon, or polyester tricot, to cotton T-shirts, using a trapunto technique. She suggests you put your drawing on tissue paper; then sew through the tissue, nylon, and cotton T-shirt. Tear away the paper and trim excess fabric around appliqué. Slash the garment on the underside where areas are to be stuffed. Use an orange stick to push in the stuffing. Catch-stitch the opening together. Add hand embroidery, or machine-stitched detail, as the design requires. Stitching gives a quilted effect to the appliquéd designs, as seen in a collection of Marilyn's shirts, Figure 4-14.

CHILDREN'S DRAWINGS
Children's drawings provide an unlimited source of design for their own clothes; Figures 4-17, 19 and 20.

Gloria McNutt, a stitcher who says she *hates* to mend, found the appliqués fun to do, especially those the children drew themselves. She recommends that you open a leg seam to simplify the stitching. The "High-Water Pants" in Figure 4-21 provide a means of lengthening outgrown jeans. The water has risen above the former hemline.

APPLIQUÉ

Sas Colby, one of the most innovative and talented designers of body coverings, uses appliqué in many ways. Figures C-17 (page 19) and C-37 (page 56) show some of her creations. Her "Vest with Medals," Figure 4-18, is a marvelous spoof that uses printed ladies, swinging fringes, and stitched ribbons. The humor with which she surrounds the symbols of heroic action are reminiscent of the "Fruit Salads" of Ruth Roach in Figures C-57 and 58 (page 107).

Christalene's magic cape in Figure 4-26 is a combination of leather, tapestry scraps, lace, and embroidery thread. Many different elements are combined, as are symbols and signs, since Christalene states that she is "a sorceress by trade and needs magical garments." The feeling that garments carry certain magical qualities is noted by many designers, in that a part of themselves becomes entwined or enmeshed in the garments they sew. Jessica Dvorak's comment is that what she most enjoys about designing clothes is "Giving them away after they are saturated with my own vibrations." Sas Colby uses a fantasy approach in her design. She says, "I like to include secret pockets and personal insignia for the wearer. Bells add another dimension, and the linings should be as lavish as the outside. I especially want the garment to impart a *magic quality* to the wearer and environment." Sas Colby's creations do indeed add magic to the lives of all who see or wear her work.

Jo Diggs, who lives and works in New Mexico, uses her stitchery, shown in Figure 4-24, to reflect her

4-38. "Beardsley Cape." One yard of 54" velvet is used in a simple drawstring, or page's, cape. The appliqué motif is drawn from a Beardsley design, and Sas Colby, the model and designer, suggests that it can also be worn as a skirt.

4-39. "Bear." Detail from an apron in which felt is slipped between the opaque fabric and the transparent material that covers it. The bear is then outlined with a running stitch. The result is a padded design with a quilted effect. By Barbara Bilovsky.

4-40. "Ruffle My Feathers." Cape and headpiece of velvet, lined in satin and taffeta. By Sas Colby.

reactions to a way of living. She says about the work, "It is my statement about living in Los Angeles for two years. It is my statement about body culture. Los Angeles is the nth degree, the logical end of the civilized world. Body culture needs no head. If you find this funny, it is because you can feel human frailty. If you find this offensive, good! Don't believe TV. Beautiful bodies don't necessarily make beautiful souls. The beautiful life makes smog." Many of Jo's costumes are shown in this book. They are beautiful garments, celebrations of the individuals for whom they are sewn.

LETTERING

"Zap" in Figure 4-41 suggests a possible way of adding words, or lettering, to clothes. The intricate shapes of letters make them somewhat difficult to appliqué with fabrics other than felt. For the dress, a single piece of felt is used for the front, another for the back, which makes assembly very simple. Join the shoulder seams first so that the neckline appliqué will overlap the seams. Finish appliqué on sleeves, dress front, and back before joining the side and underarm seams, as it is always easier to appliqué on a flat surface.

Numerous other examples in this chapter show appliquéd clothes suggesting the tremendous variety of possibilities within the reaches of this technique. Many of the articles in other chapters show appliqué in combination with embroidery, printing, or stuffing.

4-41. "Zap." Felt appliqué on felt allows for intricate shapes, such as those used in lettering. Ribbons hang free beneath the appliquéd star in a dress which seems destined for Wonder Lady, or a reader of tarot cards. By Jean Ray Laury.

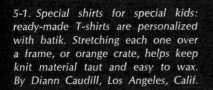

5-1. Special shirts for special kids: ready-made T-shirts are personalized with batik. Stretching each one over a frame, or orange crate, helps keep knit material taut and easy to wax. By Diann Caudill, Los Angeles, Calif.

5. Tie-Dye and Batik

There must be few craftsmen, teachers or stitchers who have not enjoyed the magic of dyed fabric. The most versatile and popular of the various dye methods are tie-dye and batik, both resist processes. This means that when the fabric is dipped in dye, those areas of the fabric that are tied off with string or painted with melted wax will resist the dye and not be colored. Much of the excitement lies in a certain unpredictability of the process. Control increases with experience, but the element of surprise remains.

Fabric Choice
Choice of fabric is important for these processes. The natural fibers—cotton, silk and linen—are traditionally the best to use. Some rayons and nylons will also dye well, but permanent-press or crease-resistant fabrics will not accept the dye. Cotton velveteen, used for the dress in Figure C-30 (page 37), is especially nice for tie-dye. Instructions included with hot- and cold-water dyes will advise you of the proper fabrics to use. It is very important to wash the fabrics before dyeing in order to remove any filler that would keep the dye from penetrating the fibers.

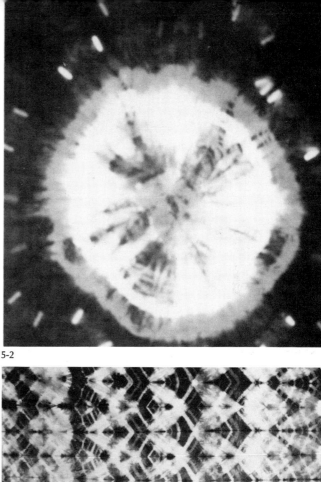

5-2

5-3   5-4

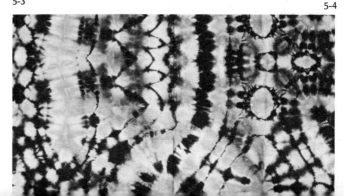

5-2. Rubber bands and clothespins acted as the resist against dye on this tie-dye fabric sample. By Joyce Aiken.

5-3. Folded and tied fabric is dyed in three colors for an allover chevron design. By Robert Erdle, Fresno, Calif.

5-4. A strong dark and light pattern is achieved by tying navy blue fabric in a random pattern and discharging it. By Judy Calandra.

TYING THE FABRIC

To tie-dye, fabric is tied, pleated, folded, sewn or knotted in such a way as to protect parts of the cloth so that they can resist the dye. These areas may be protected with string, rubber bands, clothespins, wooden blocks, sewing thread or anything else that will hold the fabric tight. The simplest of these are rubber bands and clothespins. Because they are easy to use and require no knot tying, children will find them good to work with. Figure 5-2 shows the detail of a tie-dye that uses rubber bands and clothespins to create the design. After they are in place, the fabric is wet thoroughly and put into simmering dye for about 30 minutes. The stronger the dye solution, the more intense will be the color. The fabric must have room enough in the dye bath to allow the dye to move easily around the cloth. After each color, the cloth is removed from the dye and rinsed in cool water until the excess dye runs out. More rubber bands and clothespins can be added to protect the new color, or the original ties can be removed to reveal the undyed fabric. The dye process is repeated until the desired result is obtained. Light colors should be dyed first; dark colors last.

Tying fabric that has been folded or pleated gives you more complex designs. The dress in Figure C-43 (page 90) is accordion-pleated and diagonally folded before being tied. As each new color is added, more areas are tied off to protect the first colors. Drawing 1 shows a diagram of the folding. The ties are made straight across the fabric. The zigzag design is achieved through the folding and tying. Figure 5-3 shows fabric tied in this manner and dyed three times.

DISCHARGE DYEING

Sometimes the color is taken out of a fabric and other color is put in. Figure 5-6 and Figure C-72

Text continues on p. 88

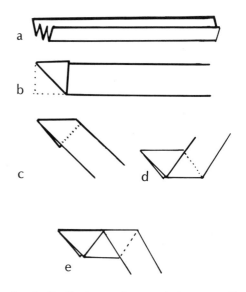

Drawing 1. To tie-dye a chevron design, accordion-pleat the fabric lengthwise (a). Lay pleated fabric flat and fold a 45° angle at one end (b). Turn fabric over and fold another 45° angle (c). Continue folding (d and e) until you have folded the entire strip of pleated fabric. Tie strings across the fabric to give a zigzag pattern in the dyeing.

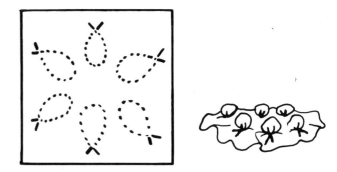

Drawing 2. Use rug thread to sew a design on the fabric you are going to dye. Do all the sewing flat, leaving 1" of the thread at start and finish of the design. When complete, gently pull threads until sewn areas are tightly closed. Tie the thread ends together.

5-6

5-5. The pattern on Suzanne Gaddy's dress is made by tie-dye technique of folding and stitching before dyeing. She is from Bakersfield, Calif.

5-6. Nine feet of red fabric are patterned by first tying and removing color and then tying and dyeing a new color. By Joyce Aiken.

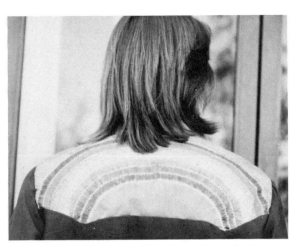

5-7. Wedding shirt, designed and sewn by Melody Steiner, was then stitched and dyed into a radiant rainbow design by Elizabeth Freeman.

5-8. Heavy thread, sewn in running stitches and pulled tight, makes the pattern in this sew-and-dye caftan. By Joyce Aiken.

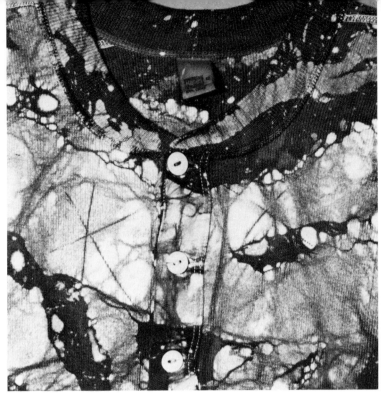

5-9. After painting areas of wax on a ready-made cotton shirt, a sharp tool was used to incise, or scratch, a design through the wax. This allowed the dye to penetrate the fabric and produced a distinct drawn line in contrast to the free crackle design.

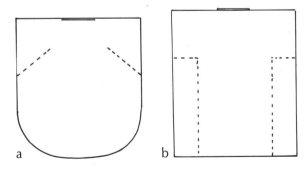

Drawing 3. Tie-dye and batik require clothing of simple design so that the dyed designs can be fully appreciated. The easiest garment to make is a caftan (a) or (b). A 45"-wide material makes a good sleeve length. Fold a fabric in half to determine its length. Then slit it on the fold line for the neck opening. Hem or bind. Stitch the sleeve line as in (a) or (b).

5-10. School children painted with melted wax on muslin fabric for their teacher, Lynn Ross, Fresno, Calif. She dyed the fabric and made it into a very special dress.

5-11. A tjanting is used for drawing lines with hot wax on fabric before dyeing. More wax is painted on to protect the first dye color, and the fabric is then dyed again in a darker color.

5-12. Hearts and dots are the border pattern for a batik shirt made of handwoven Mexican cotton. By Joyce Aiken.

(page 110) show a red chiffon fabric that is discharge-dyed. Areas are tied off to protect the red fabric before it is put into hot color remover. When the exposed fabric turns white, or off-white, the material is rinsed and more tying takes place. Some of the red fabric is exposed and some of the white tied off. The fabric is dyed a second color—blue. This gives the result of red, white, blue and violet. The navy blue fabric in Figure 5-4 is tied in a random pattern, discharged, rinsed and left without adding another color. This simple process gives a strong and interesting pattern. Figure C-29 (page 37) shows a white cotton undershirt dyed a blue base color; then tied, discharged, and finally tied and dyed red.

STITCH-AND-DYE

The seamstress who is expert at running stitch will find a potential for a more controlled design with stitch-and-dye. The novice at sewing will find a technique that gives her new kinds of patterns with which to experiment. Shapes are sewn with heavy sewing thread to make the design. When sewing is finished, each thread is pulled tight and tied securely; see Drawing 2. This holds the fabric tight and acts as protection for the cloth. Figure 5-8 and Figure C-40 (page 90) show the sewn-line design on a caftan made of Si Bonne lining fabric. A combination of sewn and folded techniques is used in the dress in Figure 5-5.

An example of more complex stitch-and-dye technique is seen in a wedding shirt in Figure 5-7. The design on the shirt, sewn and dyed by Elizabeth Freeman, shows the control of an expert craftsman. Figures C-3 and 7 (Frontispiece) show Elizabeth Freeman's superb designs in color, and they point up her ability and patience in working with a difficult approach to tie-dye.

5-13. Batik design in two colors fills the front and back of a silk cape by Joyce Aiken.

BATIK

The art of batik is as old as that of tie-dye—and just as exciting. It is like opening a present and discovering a treasure when you see the unexpected results of dyeing.

Batik requires some ability with a paint brush or a drawing tool, but the process is easily learned. The design is drawn on the cloth with melted wax. Where the wax penetrates the cloth, it resists the dye and protects the fabric color. Paraffin crazes easily and gives the design a strong crackle effect. The cotton undershirt in Figure 5-9 was waxed over most of the surface. The pattern was achieved when some areas were exposed to dye and the waxed areas folded to result in crackle. The addition of beeswax to the paraffin increases the adherence of the wax to the fabric and causes less crackle.

Wax is flammable, so precautions shold be taken when melting it. An old electric frying pan or a deep-fat fryer is ideal for keeping wax at a constant temperature. If these are not available, a pan or a large coffee can with a few inches of water in the bottom will hold and heat a smaller can of wax without exposing it directly to the burner. The wax must be hot enough to penetrate the fabric, or it will flake off and you will lose your design.

With careful supervision, children can do batik. Figure 5-10 shows teacher Lynn Ross in a dress she dyed and made after her kindergarten class painted with wax on a length of fabric. The stiff bristle brushes the children are accustomed to using are ideal for batik. Their drawings reflect their interests: suns, houses, trees. What an exciting way for children and teacher to work on a project together.

A tjanting is a very helpful tool for batik. It is a metal bowl, mounted on a wooden handle, and it has a fine spout from which hot wax is drawn out

5-14. "Cloud Shirt." Lauren Zolot of Pasadena, Calif., combines fine line and broad areas of color in a batik on a cotton undershirt.

40

41

42

43

44

45

46

47

48

49

50

51

52

C-40. Lining fabric, used the full 45" width, drapes softly in this caftan designed and modeled by Joyce Aiken. A sew-and-dye process is used for the delicate scroll design.

C-41. Dye painting and quilting are beautifully merged in this vest, designed and modeled by Lenore Davis, Buffalo, N. Y.

C-42. Patterned fabrics in bright colors combine and complement each other in this folk dress. By Charlotte Patera.

C-43. Repeat designs and regular patterns are easily achieved with the tie-dye process. In this dress, Joyce Aiken added scarlet, cerise, and navy blue to white silk.

C-44. A three-dimensional creation of patterns and textures takes form over the body of Phyllis Neufeld, Modesto, Calif., who designed and crocheted the dress.

C-45. What started out as a patchwork quilt ended up as a dress! After finishing a dozen appliqué blocks, designer Jean Ray Laury decided she would rather wear the blocks. They are pieced in such a way that the washable cotton velveteen blocks can later follow their true destiny and end up as a quilt.

C-46. Felt appliqué on felt is fast, easy, and colorful. Running stitch adds a textural detail. By Jean Ray Laury.

C-47. "Sumac Dress." Appliqué blocks are pieced together with solid colors to make a patchwork section of a dress. Sleeves use the same blocks in a smaller size. Mexican cottons are blind-stitched for appliqué, then joined by machine. By Jean Ray Laury.

C-48. This patchwork cape, reminiscent of the Pied Piper of Hamlin, is a combination of colored leathers. Scraps are glued together with Barge Cement until they make material large enough to cut into a cape pattern. Holes are punched around the bottom edge, and yarn is tied through. The yarns are then knotted into macramé fringe. By Bets Barnard.

C-49. "Hail to Thee Blithe Spirit." Sas Colby's magnificent quilted, appliquéd, and fringed cape comes to life when it is worn. Lights play over the velvets, and fringes move.

C-50. A felt dress, simply cut, is decorated with whipstitched felt appliqué. A special party motivated Barbara Kensler of Eugene, Ore., to design the dress.

C-51. A velvet vestment, lined in glossy red satin, is worn by Rev. Phillip Kimble for special services. The garment is appliquéd both front and back. By Jean Ray Laury.

C-52. If clothes reflect the mood of the wearer, the work in any office would be made lighter by this dazzling coat. By Simone Gad, Los Angeles, Calif.

5-15

in a continuous line. The scarf in Figure 5-11 shows the line quality obtainable when using a tjanting. A combination of fine lines and solid wax areas is seen in the T-shirt in Figure 5-14.

Cold-water dyes (such as Craftool or Procion) must be used with batik. Craftool dyes are safe for children to use. Procion dyes produce vibrant color and are permanent after the dye is heat set. Follow the manufacturer's directions for the dye you use. After each dyeing, the wax is removed, or more wax is added to the fabric. Color is built up as in tie-dye, with some areas remaining undyed and others mixing to make new colors. Figure 5-13 and Figure C-22 (page 19) show a two-color batik—the first color, a warm olive green; the second color, a pink orange. The combination of these two makes the background color burgundy.

When colors are set, the wax is removed with heat. One method of setting color and removing wax is to place the cloth between clean paper (paper towels) and iron until the wax melts and is absorbed into the paper. Another method is to boil the fabric. The color is set and the wax melted out during the process. If the cloth and water are left to cool, the wax floats to the top, hardens, and can be lifted off in a sheet. Any trace of wax left in the fabric can be removed by dry cleaning.

5-15. Bright suns shine from the back and sleeves of this batik caftan made with rectangles and triangles of fabric. By Lynn Ross.

5-16. Birds are drawn in melted wax on unbleached muslin. The cloth is dyed blue, waxed entirely, and dyed black for crackle effect. By Elizabeth Fuller, Claremont, Calif.

6. Leather

Changes of textures in clothing are not only visually pleasant, but are inviting for their tactile qualities. Few materials offer a more pleasurable touch than fur. Leather has a character all its own, with its suppleness, odors and sensuous qualities. The combination of fur and smooth leather gives the designer an opportunity to explore these qualities in each and to work with relief pattern and texture.

NATURAL SKIN

It is very tempting to use a skin, uncut and natural, with its markings and edges left as part of the design. Sometimes a minimum amount of altering is required in order to make the skins wearable. A slit cut for the head, as in Figure 6-3, is all that is necessary to make the skin into a poncho. The uneven edge becomes an important decorative element. It is not unlike the caveman's solution to a simple garment. Two sheepskins in Figure 6-4 wrap around the body and are joined by hand sewing. Either of these ponchos could later be cut into more sophisticated patterns.

Natural and sheared sheepskins combine nicely with other skins, or with their own reverse side, for textural changes. An interesting pattern is achieved by the textures of the skins in the jacket in Figure 6-8. Adding to the pattern is the design of the stitching as it joins the fur and leather. Text continues on p. 98

6-1. Leather is an ageless and timeless material, and one that is practical enough for ranch work but elegant enough for special occasions. Mason, of Topanga, Calif., combines leather with other fabrics for a resplendent costume that seems both durable and decorative.

6-2. Natural and sheared sheepskins combine in this handsome jacket by Steven Burke, San Gabriel, Calif.

6-3

6-4

6-3. An easy and natural way to use a leather skin is to cut an opening in the center for your head. The uneven edge adds interest. By Jean Ray Laury.

6-4. This poncho was made from two pieces of sheared sheepskin sewn together by hand with heavy carpet thread. The wool hides the stitches. By Joyce Aiken.

6-5. The functional leather-strip stitching on this vest is also an important part of the design. By Troy Nerney, Topanga, Calif.

6-6. Dyed suede scraps were cut and appliquéd on a leather vest by Jackie Vermeer.

6-7. Cross-stitches make an attractive pattern on the sleeve of this leather jacket by Mason.

6-8. Sheared and unsheared sheepskins are used with split leather. Note the shaping of fur pieces in the yoke and the pattern-effect of the stitching. By Steven Burke of San Gabriel, Calif.

6-9. Fringe adds texture and interest to this simple leather dress by Kent L. Child, Aromas, Calif.

6-10. Rivets of various sizes stud this jacket and pants with a shiny reflective pattern of dots. By Doug Hansen.

6-7

6-8

6-9

6-10

6-11. *Detail of skirt closure, with flower shapes accenting the hook loops. By Peggy Handrick, Fresno, Calif.*

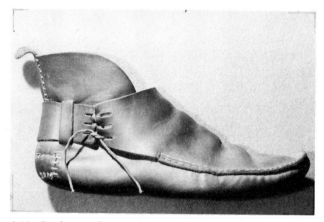

6-12. *Gordon Brofft of Brookdale, Calif., makes use of lacing and slits to form this soft, comfortable shoe.*

METHODS OF JOINING

The thickness of leather often dictates the method of putting a garment together. Seams, or joinings, in leather can become part of the design if they are treated with some concern. Figure 6-13 shows a detail of the joining of leather by overlapping edges. Slits are punched through both pieces of leather and laced with a strip of leather. The vest in Figure 6-5 is made of fragile doeskins and is laced in this manner to protect the seams from tearing. The ends of the lacing can be knotted on the outside and left to show, or they can be riveted in place. Gordon Brofft recommends that you design clothes most suitable for leather—jumpers, vests or dresses of simple cut and a minimum number of seams.

An ingenious method of adjusting the size of a leather skirt is seen in Figure 6-14. The rectangular shape of leather at the bottom of the skirt goes under the laced and riveted section in the upper part. The lacing can be loosened or tightened to fit the wearer.

Edges of leather do not have to be turned under unless added strength is desired. Fringe adds softness to a garment and sometimes covers seams, as in Figure 6-9. Holes punched along the edge of leather finish and decorate it like embroidery, as in Figure 6-18.

Leather cement is often strong enough to hold leather pieces together without additional sewing. The cape in Figure C-48 (page 90) is made of leather scraps glued together with Barge Cement. The only stitching is on the shoulder seams. Wool yarns give added luxury to the cape as a long fringe drops from the edge of the leather.

CLEANING LEATHER

If leather is treated with some respect, it can be washed without harm. The child's vest in Figure 6-6

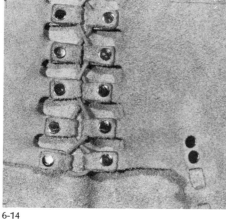

6-14

6-13. Leather vest (detail). Gordon Brofft used a punched edge and flat lacing to add a detail that is both structural and decorative.

6-14. Beautiful detailing in a leather skirt by Gordon Brofft. The rectangle of leather at the bottom of the skirt is one piece that carries up under the laced section and allows the lacing to be loosened to adjust to the size of the wearer.

6-15. Sun shines in leather appliqué on the bottom of blue jeans. By Patti Rague, Culver City, Calif.

6-16. A medley of textures and colors emerges from the patchwork pieces in a leather vest by Sandi Fox, Los Angeles.

6-17. Leather pants made by Mason, Topanga, Calif., use only leather strips to join seams, tears, and closures.

6-13

6-15

6-16

6-17

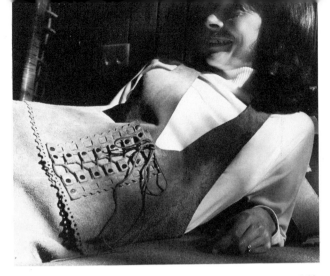

6-18. The closure for this leather vest by Gordon Brofft makes a complex pattern of thong, rivets, and leather shapes.

6-19. Leather dress by Gordon Brofft uses buckles and flat lacing for closing and decorating the garment.

6-20. The softness of deerskin made this dress easy to sew. By Jan McAweeney, Fresno, Calif.

6-19

6-20

is made of suede, and when it is soiled, it is hand-washed in tepid water with soap. One leather merchant suggests that you care for suede the way you would care for your own skin—using soap, not detergents, and avoiding scalding water or sudden changes of water temperature from hot to cold. The leather appliqué on the blue jeans in Figure 6-15 has withstood the test of washing. Commercial products are available in liquid or in spray form to protect the surface of leather. Leather may also be dry-cleaned if you find a cleaning establishment which specializes in leather. Many leather craftsmen feel the skins are enriched when the used surfaces take on a patina of small scratches, marrings and even spots.

RIVETS AND LACING

Doug Hansen, like most students, prefers to wear one-of-a-kind clothes. His decorated jacket and pants, Figure 6-10, are a spoof on motorcycle garb. Doug draws his design on the leather and jeans material with chalk before applying the rivets, which are available at leather stores in shapes of stars, diamonds, and rounds.

The most basic and natural construction in leather can sometimes be the most handsome. The pants in Figure 6-17 have side seams joined with fine leather thongs tied and left as fringe. Round braided leather laces the front closure. A horse blanket lines the leather jacket in Figure 6-7. The cross-stitch lacing on the sleeves is especially attractive, and thong ends are left as fringes along the seam.

Once you have got over the fear of cutting into a beautiful skin or fur, you'll find working with leather a real joy. Few tools are necessary—a strong pair of scissors, a hole punch, a needle—and you can start. You may find that it's easier than working with fabric.

6-21 The elegant hitchhiker, with a collection of handcrafted leather bags, has a place for everything and a few places left over. The hiker and designer is Sherwin Strull.

6-24

6-22. *What could be more luxurious than crawling into a sleeping bag covered with fur and latched yarns? By Joyce Aiken.*

6-23 and 24. *An elegant sleeping bag is encased in deerskin and fur. Unrolled sleeping bag reveals handwoven top in textured yarns. By Yvonne Porcella.*

6-22

7. Non-Clothing

Perhaps we all retain a touch of the Puritan ethic of thrift which lets us particularly enjoy making something from nothing. Recycled clothes, or renovated wear, are fun because they challenge us creatively and are ecologically satisfying. An old slogan which came from England in World War II goes, "Use it up, wear it out, make it do, or do without." It allows for an adventurous approach in using old things, and it gives attention to the clever, or thrifty, use of castoffs. It has become fashionable to "rerun" clothes. Many of the clothes in this book make use of old things. Blue denim work shirts and blue jeans seem the most popular. In this chapter, you will find examples of clothes made from blankets, scarves, and tablecloths—things not originally intended to be worn.

Necktie skirts have been around for a long time, but they are always interesting and amusing. The patterns in the ties practically let you name the year in which the ties were first worn, as in Figure 7-2.

OLD TABLECLOTHS

The current appreciation for needlework puts a special value on crocheted, woven, and embroidered pieces for whatever purpose they may originally have been made. Lace tablecloths, having been displaced by plastic mats or natural wood tables, are being pulled out of bottom drawers and looked at

7-1. "Drawn-Work Dress." Folded in half and joined at the sides, the embroidery and the drawn work in this linen cloth show to great advantage over a dark garment.

7-2. "Necktie Skirt." An amusing skirt offers a possibility for recycling old neckties. While the idea of the skirt is not new, ties keep changing in width, pattern, and color so that each skirt records another passing fad in what was often the only bit of color worn with the gray flannel suit. From Turtle Bay Trading Co., Los Angeles, Calif.

7-3. A tablecloth, folded crosswise, becomes a dress. This one was made as shown in the drawing. By Jean Ray Laury.

again. Figure C-74 (page 110) shows a dress made from one of these. Drawing 1 (page 113) shows a simple way of sewing such a dress.

An old lace cloth provides the material for a new lace dress. It is sometimes easier on the conscience to cut a cloth that already has a tear in it, or a stubborn stain. For a dress, the tear can be mended or the spot covered, and when the fabric falls in folds while being worn, minor imperfections are lost. It is sometimes possible to cut out dress pieces in such a way that spots or tears can be avoided.

This chapter shows various examples of clothes made from finished runners, tablecloths, covers, or dresser scarves. Few require any cuts to be made in the lace material.

BLANKET DRESSES
Blankets give you a good big piece of fabric to use. They are often worn in spots, or torn or damaged. Large areas are left, which are still usable. The army surplus blanket in Figure 7-15 is enriched with felt appliqué. The blankets used for the cape in Figure 7-11 were received as a wedding gift a number of years ago and had haunted Penneye Kurtela. Sentimental value made it difficult to pass them along. She found no need to use them and little room to store them, so she cut and appliquéd them into a cape. The blankets are now being used and enjoyed for their warmth, beauty, and sentimental value.

Penneye says, "If you want to make something, first look around the house to see what material is available. Everyone has something he doesn't use, but refuses to throw away. This is a good place to start creating the unique body covering. The cost is nil and the reward is great."

Some other uses of old blankets are seen in Figures 7-7, 12, and 14.

7-4. An old brown silk piano scarf, with embroidery and macramé fringe, makes a great dress. Originally a large square, half is used for the sleeves and the other half for the front and back. Sleeves are cut so that the fringed edge of the scarf falls at the back of the sleeves. By Jean Ray Laury.

C-53. Traditional patchwork and embroidery combine in a brilliant textured skirt. By L. S. Witt, San Jose, Calif.

C-54. Palm trees sway over a satin sky in this padded and stuffed bib. By Reta Miller, Newberg, Ore.

C-55. An old umbrella frame provided a base for this lacy, openwork crochet. By Mark D. Law, Pomona, Calif.

C-56. A rip in his pants got Tom Logan, Fresno, Calif., started on embroidery. It grew until bugs and butterflies covered a vine that entwines one pants leg.

C-57. "Fruit Salad." One of a series of salads designed to doll up men's jackets or coats. By jewelry designer Ruth S. Roach, Naples, Fla.

C-58. "Good-Conduct Medals." A tongue-in-cheek comment by Ruth S. Roach pokes gentle fun at identification tags worn at conventions and as club pins.

C-59. Satin stitch and outline stitch encircle the legs of a man's blue denim pants. By Jean Ray Laury.

C-60. Velveteen appliqués form a landscape around the bottom of these pants. By Jean Ray Laury.

C-61. Detail of shadow work. A transparent fabric, such as organza, is placed over colored fabrics and stitched. By Barbara Bilovsky, Fresno, Calif.

C-62. Printed lettering on a feed sack is emphasized by outlining with a permanent marking pen. By Jean Ray Laury.

C-63. Cotton fabrics are easily blind-stitched to uncut corduroy pants. By Jean Ray Laury.

C-64. An invitation to a mountain wedding led designer Jean Ray Laury to patch and embroider these pants for her son.

C-65. A circle of cut-through appliqué brightens the bib front of an apron. By Jody House, Davis, Calif.

C-66. Five layers of fabric in this appliqué add weight and body to the bib of a jumper. By Jean Ray Laury.

C-67. The exquisite embroidery by Joanne Derr, Spring Valley, Calif., makes a magical garden of denim pants.

C-68. A velveteen rainbow fills the blue sky of these corduroy pants.

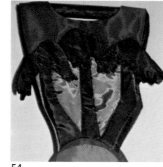

54

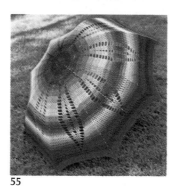

55

56

58

59

60

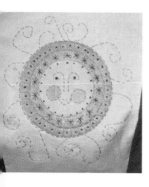

62

63

64

66

67

68

7-5. A diamond-shaped tablecloth is slit in the center to provide a neck opening. Edges are tacked together under the arms to hold the poncho in place. By Jean Ray Laury.

7-6. A combination of dresser scarf, doilies, and crochet made a lacy dress, or shirt, for a girl. By Jean Ray Laury.

7-7. *Careful planning and simple cuts turned a 15-year-old stadium blanket into a new fringed plaid coat. See Drawing 2 for simple cutting method. By Patti Handley, Fresno, Calif.*

7-8. *"Poncho." A small crocheted tablecloth is cut in the center to make a poncho. The raw edge at the neckline is machine stitched and then bound. By Jean Ray Laury.*

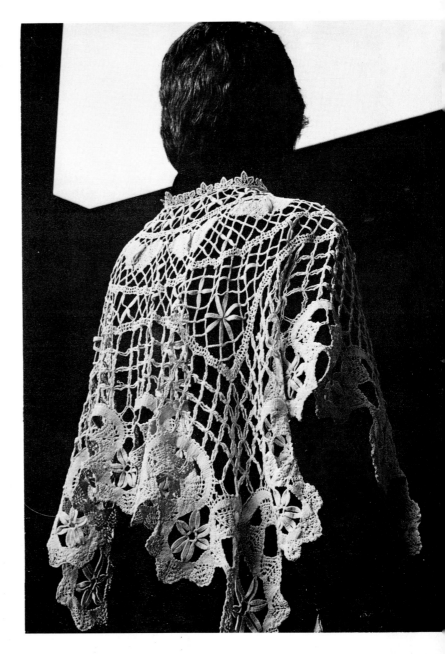

69

70

71

72

73

74

75

76

77

78

79

C-69. A tweed coat, covered with embroidery and appliqué, loses its traditional look and sparkles with color. By L. S. Witt.

C-70. Yvonne Porcella adds wrapped cords, ending in tassels, to the back of a bib neck piece. A friend finds it easier to see you go when you leave him with a vision of swinging, bouncing, colorful action.

C-71. A large leather purse receives special treatment with the addition of a needlepoint square covered with bugs and things. By Yvonne Porcella.

C-72. A nine-foot panel of red chiffon was dye-treated in two steps. The first involved removing color (tie-and-discharge), followed by tie-and-dye. The single panel is worn as a flowing scarf. By Joyce Aiken.

C-73. Cotton velveteens are easy to sew and to appliqué, using a blind stitch. Basic pullover can be cut without a pattern. By Jean Ray Laury.

C-74. An old, no-longer-used lace tablecloth is made into this delicate and detailed dress. The center panel of the cloth forms a decorative neck line, and the border forms a hem pattern. By Jean Ray Laury.

C-75. Mexican cotton is stacked for the exquisite detail by using a cut-through technique. The appliqué dress was designed and sewn by Gloria McNutt, Visalia, Calif.

C-76. Lettering is whipstitched felt-on-felt. The rolled edges at the skirt bottom and sleeve ends are stuffed with Dacron so that they are stiff enough to hold their shapes. By Jean Ray Laury.

C-77. K. Lee Manuel transforms the wearer of her clothes into something special with her beautiful painted and padded creations.

C-78. K. Lee Manuel started designing clothes "to elevate the body and the individual to something aesthetically and visually exciting—like a rare bird—a flower in a field of grass." Her "Peacock Cape" shows the extent to which she carries out her goals.

C-79. Leftover yarns of all weights were beautifully embroidered on to an old army blanket by Esther Feldman, Los Angeles, Calif.

7-9. A Japanese table runner, richly embroidered with silk and gold thread, is made into an elegant dress, modeled by the scurrying designer. By folding the fabric in half (lengthwise), the top is cut and fitted. The sides are left slit, partly for the dramatic effect and partly to make it possible to walk in the narrow skirt. The orange satin lining picks up the orange in the brocade and also protects the wearer from the scratchy metallic threads. By Patti Handley.

7-10. The cape, made from a lace tablecloth, is gathered at the neck and tied in the front. A stiff fabric lining is sewn into the edge to keep the gathers upright. All finished edges of the cloth are used, and no cuts are made into the lace. By Joyce Aiken.

7-11. Two old wool blankets were cut to make this cape with boldly designed shapes cut from felt. Wool-yarn blanket stitches outline the appliqué. By Penneye Kurtela, Fresno, Calif.

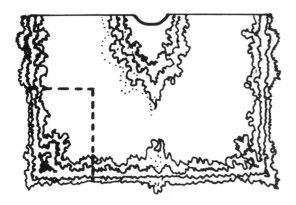

Drawing 1. A lace tablecloth, folded in half, forms the basis for a dress. Sections may be cut out of the corners, leaving a sleeve shape and providing material for a collar. If a small tablecloth is used, a top, or pullover, could be made. A larger cloth might be dress length. Either way, a finished decorative edge eliminates the necessity of hemming.

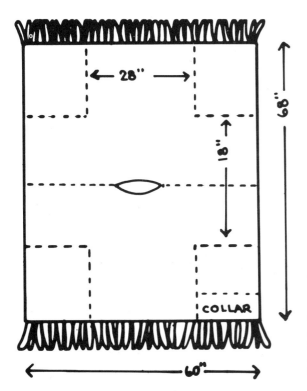

Drawing 2. A fringed blanket, afghan, or lap robe can be made into a simple coat by cutting as shown. Blankets of different sizes and proportions can be used to make full-length coats. Fold your material and hold it up to yourself to check for size.

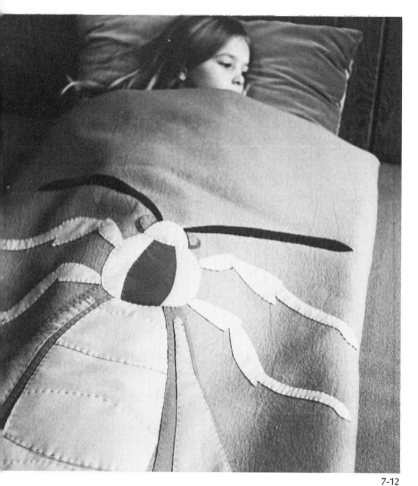

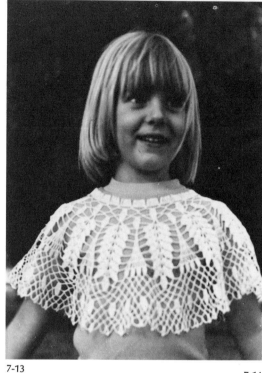

7-12

7-12. A giant insect, cut from felt, is appliquéd onto an old wool blanket. The blanket is wrapped around a lightweight sleeping bag and then joined to the bag at the top and bottom, as well as down the seam, where the edges of the blanket meet. By Jean Ray Laury.

7-13. Large "found" doily, which was torn in the center, was cut to make a delicate lacy collar. By Jean Ray Laury.

7-14. An Irish blanket and two striped rebozos from Guatemala provide handwoven material for these simple skirts. The rebozos are folded in half, cut, and sewn up the sides. Waists are gathered. The blanket, a lap-robe size, is cut away at one edge, leaving the fringe at the bottom. By Jean Ray Laury.

7-15

7-15. "Alison's Blanket." A tomboy's blanket, with felt appliqué. The lettering serves to decorate the Army blanket, and also to identify it. By Jean Ray Laury.

7-16. Detail shows the overcast stitch used on the felt. By Jean Ray Laury.

7-16

8-1. Patchwork with pieces of old blue jeans offers a rich range of soft blues in this cape by stitchery artist Jody House.

8. Patchwork

Patchwork is a method of fabricating, or forming, materials by collecting and joining together many scraps or patches. The patchwork may be sewn in either of two basic ways—piecing or patching. In piecing, the scraps of fabric are placed face to face and joined at one edge so that an area of fabric is gradually created. The pieces can be strips, bands, squares, rectangles, or some other geometric shape. In patching, the fabrics are made into a collage, one over another, and usually there is a garment, or a large piece of fabric, to which the patches are added. Both of these ways of working are referred to as patchwork. An example of piecing can be seen in Figure C-47 (page 90), and patching in Figure C-53 (page 107).

COLLAGE
Patching, a kind of collage approach, allows for rich composition to develop in textures and colors. Patches may be padded and stuffed to give a sculptured surface, or they may be kept flat to suggest a single layer of material.

The way in which patches are joined becomes a part of the design. L. S. Witt's skirt, referred to above, uses the embroidery stitches of old-fashioned quilts to exaggerate the seam lines of the patches. The result is a rich and complex collection of lines and colors.

8-2. A plain white panel is inset with the strong patterns of prints in a patchwork skirt by Margaret Vaile of Atherton, Calif.

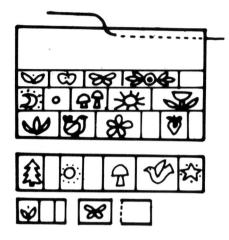

Drawing 1. Appliqué blocks of various sizes can be joined in straight rows. No tapering is required if the skirt is then gathered at the top.

Drawing 2. To use appliqué and patchwork on a tapered skirt, each block must be tapered. The patchwork must be kept parallel to the bottom edge of the skirt.

A good approach for the beginner is one which joins square or rectangular blocks, avoiding diagonals and bias cuts. Figure C-45 (page 90) shows a patchwork skirt of appliquéd blocks which are easily joined. It is helpful to lay out a pattern (whether a printed pattern or another garment) so that you can determine whether or not blocks need to be tapered. To avoid tapering, a skirt must be cut straight and gathered at the top. If a skirt is to be fitted, then the blocks must be placed parallel to the hem and tapered towards the top. Drawings 1 and 2 show how this is done. If a skirt is cut nearly straight, it may be possible to use the blocks straight, tapering only at the side seams.

The skirt in drawings 3 and 4 shows patches joined in bands (pieced) and gathered at the top. When sewing, be sure to press all seams the same way.

This is a simple kind of skirt to assemble, since all pieces are joined in straight lines of sewing.

CRAZY-QUILT TECHNIQUE

The patchwork skirt in Figure 8-2 uses a crazy-quilt approach. Margaret Vaile uses a preshrunk lightweight cotton for backing and sews patches to it. The first patch is sewn flat. A second patch is placed over the first, face-to-face, and sewn at one edge. It is then opened and pressed. That system is continued, overlapping one block on another, until enough backing has been patched to make one section of the skirt. She sometimes cuts the skirt parts, or gores, from the backing and thus patches only the exact size needed. This makes possible the kind of color change noted in Figure 8-3.

STRIPS

The vest in Figure 8-4 is assembled from strips of fabric. The strips are cut from pieced fabrics, as

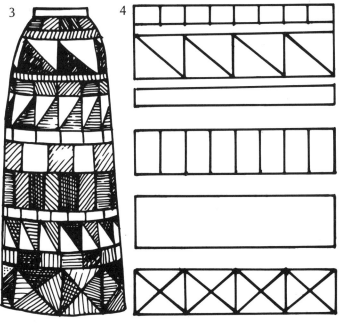

Drawing 3. Piecing is most easily done in bands or strips. The strips, requiring only straight lines of stitching, can then be joined.

Drawing 4. Piecing is done in strips, then strips are joined as in Drawing 3.

shown in Drawing 5. Sally Garoutte, the designer, admits that she hates sewing, but she likes wearing the finished clothes. Since truly unique garments are expensive, she is willing to sew. She considers making clothes a problem in "applied topology," since one must continuously allow for the hills and valleys of a figure. The pieced vest, while simple to sew, is still a unique garment, rich in patchwork detail.

Yvonne Porcella's use of piecing creates clothing that is complex, strong, and beautiful. Figure C-18 (page 19) shows one of her stunning dresses. Others are in Figures 8-5 and 6.   Text continues on p. 124

8-3. This skirt, combining strips, blocks, and patches of all sizes, is reminiscent of the traditional crazy quilt. Margaret Vaile has graded colors from strong dark ones at the base to light ones at the top.

8-4. Strips of knitted and woven wools are joined to make a single piece of material. The piece is then cut into diagonal bands and joined to straight strips to form the pattern. By Sally Garoutte of Mill Valley, Calif.

Drawing 5. Strips of fabric are joined, then cut into diagonals. They are then reassembled in alternating rows to produce a chevron pattern.

8-5. By skillfully combining patchwork, prints, colors, ribbons, and weaves, Yvonne Porcella created a dress of rich pattern and variety.

8-6

8-6. The cuff and sleeve show a collection of pieced fabrics in another dress modeled by the designer, Yvonne Porcella.

8-7 and 8. A nursing shirt sports piecework pockets which drop down over the cutout sections underneath! Though it was made in jest, any nursing mother can see its real value. Designed for Ruth Law by Frank Laury.

8-7

8-8

8-9

8-10

8-9. Detail. A rich pattern is created with cotton fabrics by overlapping the individual yo-yos.

8-10. Detail. Lining material, partially transparent, shows the construction, hemming, and folding of the yo-yos.

8-11. A pieced quilt top, which never quite reached the quilting frame, was used as material for this dress. The eight-pointed stars, which formed the major part of the design, were used on sleeves and back. By Jean Ray Laury.

8-12. Detail of Cathedral Window block. By Helen and Catherine Winter, Oakland, Calif.

8-13. Quilt blocks from a thrift store were joined together to make a pattern for the sleeves and skirt. Blocks of blue-and-white print were combined with a pale blue lightweight denim. By Jean Ray Laury.

8-11

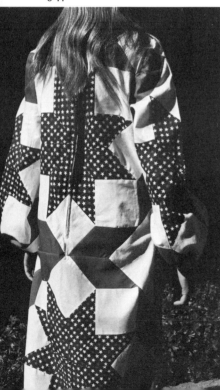

8-12

8-13

8-14. An appliqué quilt (unquilted) inspired the design of this dress. A series of blocks was joined for the skirt, with part of the border pattern beneath that. On the dress top, one unit of the border design outlines the neck line. By Joyce Aiken.

8-15. Bands of color at the borders of the quilt were used for the front panel of the dress in bright red, white, and blue (back view in Figure 8-11).

8-16. A cotton dress incorporates a panel of folded and stitched fabric made in a traditional Cathedral Window quilt pattern. By Helen and Catherine Winter.

8-17. Yo-yos, which are stitched circles of fabric, are joined here to make a floor-length vest. Assorted materials in a close color range are used. By Edith Moellering Malpas, Oakland, Calif.

8-18. Old blue jeans were taken apart and reassembled to make this jumper and skirt. Pockets, which had been removed, were appliquéd back onto the garment. By Bea Slater.

8-19. Detail of Figure 8-1. Overall buttons, with embroidery, form flower centers in the decorative blocks around the neckline. The fly front of jeans suggests a buttoned opening for the cape. By Jody House.

QUILTS INTO CLOTHES

If you are fortunate enough to have an old pieced quilt, especially one that is unquilted, you have ample patchwork for a dress. Several possible ways of incorporating either blocks or tops are shown in Figures 8-11, 13, and 14.

Other methods of quilt-making, such as appliqué or embroidery, will also lend themselves to clothing. A quilt which is worn, torn, or stained may be cut up and made into a garment. If it is already quilted, the material may be a little heavy. A skirt, vest, poncho, or simple pullover would be suitable. However, set-in sleeves, or a collar, might be more difficult to sew because of the thickness of the quilt.

Sas Colby's cape in Figure C-39 (page 56) is a beautiful example of a quilt-patch design put to a new use. She has capitalized on the shape of the individual blocks for a dramatic edge design.

8-20. *Cathedral Window vest, in which brightly colored fabrics are set into a white background. By Phyllis Hall.*

8-21. *The pieced quilt blocks were joined in a row; then sewn to a solid-colored fabric. Dress parts were cut from that fabric so that blocks edged the skirt and sleeves. By Jean Ray Laury.*

8-22. *Detail of patchwork skirt by L. S. Witt, showing the embroidery stitches used over the patchwork lines.*

8-20

TRADITIONAL PATTERNS

A panel using the Cathedral Window quilt patch is set into a dress seen in Figure 8-16. The elaborately treated blocks of stitched and folded fabrics are used in contrast to the plain weave of a solid-colored dress. Another example of the Cathedral Window block is used in the vest shown in Figure 8-20.

The Yo-Yo, another traditional quilt form, uses a circle of fabric which is cut and hemmed. Then the sewing thread is pulled tight so that the circle gathers in to form a pouch. It is flattened and can be joined to another circle. In the full-length vest, Figure 8-17, the yo-yos are sewn at the edges where they meet. Another method of joining, which makes a stronger fabric, is that of overlapping the circles. this method of overlapping, as well as the construction of the circles, is seen in Figure 8-10.

8-21

BLUE-JEANS PATCHES

The patchwork used in Jody House's cape, Figure 8-1, uses squares all identical in size. The variety in color results from the age of the various blue jeans which were salvaged.

Blue jeans have a great appeal to stitchers from teen-age on up. Perhaps it is because the more the material is used, the softer it gets in color and texture. All people who wear Levis and denims seem to part with the worn ones only with great reluctance. There is also something very unpretentious

8-22

C-80 and 81. Joanna Gray, a teacher from Claremont, Calif., helps her students make spectacular footgear out of the most unfashionable, or out-of-date, shoes. She offers them inspiration, paints, and Salvation Army footwear for these spectacular results.

C-82. Detachable cuffs of brightly stitched needlepoint add a brilliant touch to an otherwise ordinary blouse. By Joyce Aiken.

C-83. For safari, golf, or street wear, acrylic-painted hats add style to any outfit! A base coat of white acrylic helps assure bright colors. By Joyce Aiken.

C-84. More old shoes, resplendent in a new coat of paint! By Joanna Gray.

C-85. These sneakers, which had almost passed their prime, are given a new lease on life with canned spray paint by Doug Hansen, Fresno, Calif. He rejuvenated the pants with acrylic paints and permanent marking pens.

C-86. Detail of Figure C-75, cut-through appliqué. By Gloria McNutt.

C-87. A magnificent companion for a traveler, this many-pocketed leather bag is the work of Sherwin Strull, Hollywood, Calif.

C-88. "From the Beach." Surely any man would enjoy having this voluptuous swimmer paddling out between his lapels! Designer Susan Morrison, Reno, Nev., says ties provide another way of using the stuffed figure at which she excels.

C-89. Designer Simone Gad personalizes each garment she makes. This regal cape for a motorcyclist flares elegantly in the wind.

C-90. Esther Feldman, a stitchery teacher, didn't wear (and didn't like) a white cardigan she owned, so she started embroidering. The sweater is now a lavish, complex collection of stitches and textures.

C-91. Lenore Davis spends much of her time doing soft sculpture. Her "Boa Man," dyed, painted, and stuffed, combines her humor and concern for three-dimensional form with something to wear.

80

81

82

83

84

85

86

87

88

90

91

and basic about them—a kind of a down-on-the-farm simplicity that everyone enjoys. Certainly the informality of life today has made it possible to appreciate denims. Figure 8-24 and 25 show some patched jeans. Others will be seen with embroidery, appliqué, or paint applied to the fabric.

Bea Slater, who was once a fashion assistant and a model, says, "If something is both practical and unique, you can wear it almost forever and still feel well dressed." Bea made her skirt and the jumper for her daughter Sammie, shown in Figure 8-18. Because she always liked clothes best when they were worn out, and never liked new things, she started making new clothes out of worn clothes. If you can't afford new clothes, or don't feel comfortable in the latest thing, then Levis patchwork may be for you! You do have to be able to wear your clothes without feeling self-conscious in them. It's easier to be different nowadays without being considered odd. Bea adds that nobody any longer expects society to "be an agreeable mass of sameness."

OTHER PATCHWORK

"Jenny Masterson's Dress," shown in detail in Figure 8-27, has a row of beaded strings, each one of which ends in a sea-urchin's spine. To attach each spine, she drills into the end; then jams a string into the drilled hole and fills it with glue. Beads are next added. The individual strings can be detached from the waist so that if you wish, you can wear the dress without the accompanying tinkling and clinking of the spines.

A more traditional use of patchwork is seen in Figure 8-22, a detail of the skirt shown in Figure C-53 (page 107). Elsa Brown's striking use of traditional pieced patchwork in a cape shown in the Introduction has a very contemporary look.

Patchwork allows the designer to use an endless variety of fabrics and colors to produce new pat-

8-23. A skier's stuffed patchwork breastplate has a single bib-shaped fabric base to which patches of felt are whip-stitched and stuffed. By Jean Ray Laury.

8-24

8-25

8-26

8-24. *Patched jeans by an anonymous designer, who wore her work to the Renaissance Faire.*

8-25. *Prints and patterns of all colors are used by Doug Hansen to patch his jeans, thus restoring their function and adding a personal touch.*

8-26. *Appliquéd flower panels are pieced together, side by side, to make the lining for this cotton velveteen drawstring cape. By Jean Ray Laury.*

8-27. *"Jenny Masterson's Dress." Though not actually patchwork, sections of the dress are pieced together from various fabrics. The highlight is the activity of the sea-urchin's spines attached at the waist. By Jo Diggs.*

terns. Scrap materials, old outgrown clothes, remnants, tablecloths—any fabric can be incorporated. The results are always satisfying and usually stunning. Most of us enjoy patchwork even more because of the nostalgic overtones. It reminds us of grandmother's quilts, or the patchwork clothes of Cinderella, or the Pied Piper of Hamlin. Perhaps David's Biblical coat-of-many-colors was itself a patchwork garment.

8-27

9-1. *This elegant necklace combines beads, leather, and metal with peacock feathers. By Lance Bowen, Fresno, Calif.*

9. Accessories

It is sometimes difficult to know when a special work has ceased to be an article of clothing and has become a game, an environment, or a work for exhibition. Practicality might eliminate some things as unwearable, but humor would demand that they be included. We all tend to be a little too stuffy at times anyway, and nothing deflates stuffiness more gently or deftly than humor. We often take our clothes and ourselves too seriously.

SHOES AND SOCKS

Socks must surely be the most mundane of all wearing apparel. But the ones in Figure 9-6 offer a bonus. The wing-tip "shoes" are silk-screened onto cotton socks. Great for people who like to pad around in their stocking feet while looking well shod!

The hand-knit socks in the Introduction allow the toes to wiggle individually—practical, comfortable, and good for the toes. The embroidered leaves of Figure 9-7 were done when a high-school girl wanted to make some personal gifts for Christmas, but was short on time *and* money. An even easier solution for decoration is the use of a permanent marking pen, or a liquid embroidery pen. They flow into cotton easily, and they are a great help if socks need to be identified or sorted. A small symbol, initial, or picture on the toe or sole will make it easy. Even a three-year-old can match the drawings.

9-2. Free crochet neck piece, incorporating feathers, is worn by the designer, Phyllis Neufeld.

Shoes, which might seem difficult to personalize, have at least a few possibilities. Figures C-80 and 81 (page 127) show some of Joanna Gray's marvelous enameled shoes. She seems to delight in adding pastoral scenes and absurd, or unlikely, surfaces to the most commonplace articles. See Figures 9-15, 9-24, and 9-28 for more of Joanna's creations. Another pair of shoes, Figure 9-10, is painted black, white, red, and green. Joanna suggests that you remove all wax from the surface of the shoe before painting, or the wax will resist the enamels and the paint will peel. Acrylic paints, or children's dye markers, will work on fabric shoes, as in Figures 9-11 and 9-12.

STUFFED SCULPTURES

M. K. Sprague, of St. Louis, Mo., a teacher and painter who also works in soft sculpture, made herself a hat of stuffed and stitched materials, Figure 9-23. With tongue hanging out, the stuffed face harangues and drapes a coy arm over the side of the hat. M.K. says the hat is a self-portrait after teaching the first week of the new semester. She is modeling the hat in the photograph, so you can judge the likeness for yourself! The hat actually just provides an elaborate excuse for doing the sculptured face.

Susan Morrison uses ties as the props on which to make her statements about figures. Figure C-88 (page 127) and Figure 9-19 show examples of her work. Using nylon stockings stuffed with Dacron fiber fill, she works her incredible creations in three-dimensional form, then attaches them to ties. Synthetic wigs are cut up for hair, and the girls are dressed with trims of lace, beads, and feathers. Both machine- and hand-sewing are used, with facial coloring added through the use of lipstick, eye shadow and rouge.

Reta Miller, from Newberg, Ore., created the marvelous pieces shown in Figures 9-3, 4, and 25. She overlays our recollections with humor, as much of

Text continues on p. 136

9-3

132

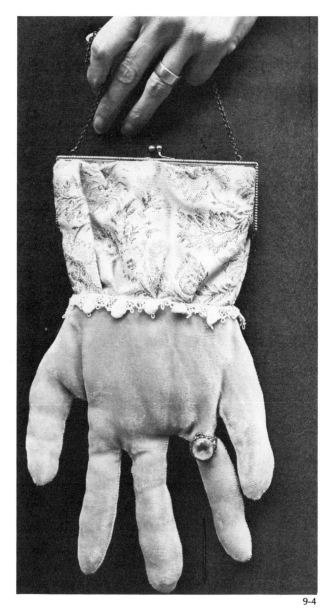

9-4

9-3 and 4. "Hand Bags." Stuffed velveteen hands emerge from cuffs which snap shut at the top to form purses. The ultimate in "hand" bags! They are especially fun to use. When your arm is dropped to your side, the hand fondles you just about at knee level. Inside the bags were placed old fountain pens, dance-program pencils, and other tidbits reminiscent of another place and time. By Reta Miller.

9-5. "Three-People Scarf." A knitted scarf, in brightly colored bands, is long enough to warm the necks of several people at one time. By Mark D. Law.

9-5

9-6

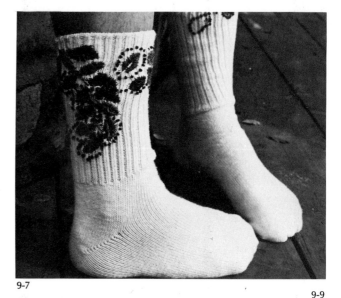

9-7

9-8

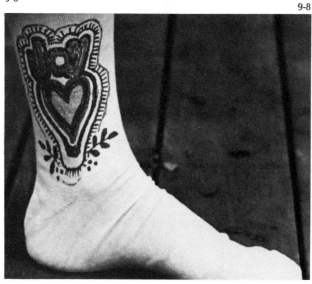

9-9

9-6. "Wing-Tip Shoes?" A silk-screen print on white socks lets you pad around in stocking feet while you appear to be more formally attired! These should be good for office work, or at least good for a laugh. House of Laurelling, Spokane, Wash.

9-7. Embroidery floss is used for satin stitches and French knots on plain white socks. These were sewn by Liz Laury, 15 years old.

9-8 and 9. Permanent marking pens add bright color to the dumbest cotton socks. By Jean Ray Laury.

9-10

9-11

9-12

9-13

9-10. An old pair of shoes, retrieved from a thrift shop, emerges with a new life under brightly colored enamel paints. By Joanna Gray.

9-11. Once shoes are painted, they are hard to part with, as evidence by Doug Hansen's sneakers. New life and color are added to this pair that were beginning to show their age.

9-12. Sneakers painted with dye markers. By Jackie Vermeer.

9-13. "Fancy Sneakers." The lowly sneaker becomes a Cinderella, appearing garbed in glittering sequins—and gold laces! For dress-up. By Becky Saiki, Clovis, Calif.

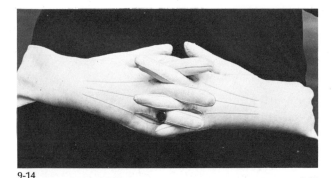

9-14

9-15

her work contains fragments of the past. One of her main problems is in finding the objects to use—antique purse closures, or doilies, or whatever—and then having the heart to use them. Reta is first a sculptress, second a painter, and third a seamstress. She says, "It just happens that I have combined these in relationship to the body. I like to make my articles lighthearted. My sculptures become cartoons, and so do the clothes I make."

BODY JEWELRY

Body jewelry is an area of such variety that we can take only a brief glimpse at some of the current ways of working. Feathers and beading have captured the imagination of many young jewelry designers. Beads and feathers are combined in Figure 9-1. Charlotte Patera uses fabric to cover various forms, which are then joined by using threads and beading. And lots of glue! See Figure 9-21.

Figures C-57 and 58 (page 107) show the work of jewelry-designer Ruth S. Roach. Her use of antique photos and advertising pins gives a cloudy, nostalgic charm to contrast with her exquisite and precise gold and silver metalwork. While knowledge of jewelry-making and stone-setting is essential, other processes used are fairly simple. Rayon and velvet ribbons are epoxied into place rather than sewn. The "Fruit Salads" were designed to doll up men's too-serious jackets or coats. She states that all "add life to a party without dazzling other people with diamonds." Having collected the photo buttons for

Text continues on p. 142

9-14. *Full-length white kid gloves, with hands stuffed, make a belt. They could hold your tummy in, or just hug you. The clasp is concealed where the gloves overlap in the back. By Ruth Law, Pomona, Calif.*

9-15. *"Peanut Necktie." Resin-coated peanuts cover a necktie for a startling effect. Joanna could lighten any faculty meeting or sales conference with this creation. By Joanna Gray.*

9-16. Delicate embroidery and French knots are sewn on the fabric before it is cut into a circle and attached to a button form. By Mary Becker.

9-17. Detail of "Good-Conduct Medals." They are shown in Figure C-58 (page 107). By Ruth Roach.

9-18. "From the Beach." Floating on her inner tube, the "baby" takes some of the austerity out of office work. She is formed from stuffed nylon hose, with stitched and painted features. By Susan Morrison.

9-19. "Frank's Tie." Made as a valentine, the very white-bodied, red-headed "doll" reposes on a red-and-white checkered tie. By Susan Morrison.

9-16

9-17

9-18

9-19

137

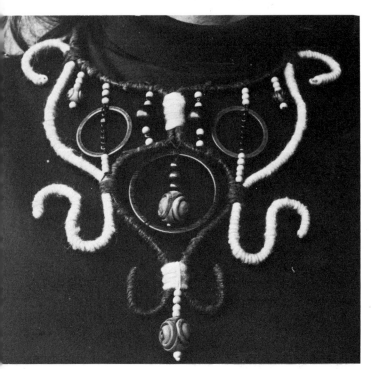

9-20

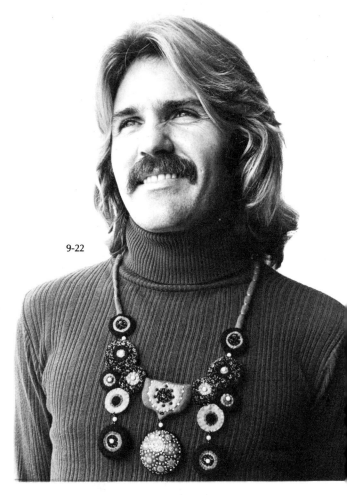

9-22

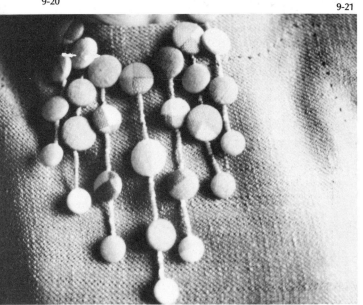

9-21

9-20. Wrapped wool, beads of various sizes, and wooden rings are worked by steady hands. Heavy wire is bent into scroll shapes first; then wrapped with wool yarns. By Robert Bowley, Montebello, Calif.

9-21. Fabric-covered button forms in bright colors make a simple, but delightful, necklace. By Charlotte Patera.

9-22. Printed materials and felts are used, highlighted with appliqué, embroidery, and stuffing in this soft jewelry piece. By Barbara Kensler.

Sticking out her tongue at all who pass, the stuffed face on this hat makes a marvelous contrast to the somewhat pompous black velvets and feathers. By M. K. Sprague, St. Louis, Mo.

9-25. "Watermelon Collar." Old embroidered panel with stitched and stuffed forms. The three-dimensional watermelons hang free at the edge of the biblike garment. While she likes her clothing to be functional and comfortable, Reta Miller also likes to add "a touch of something unusual."

9-24. Peanut hat and belt. The designer obviously enjoys wearing her own creations. By Joanna Gray.

9-26. *Crocheted bib (or breastplate). Hard-finished cords and soft yarns are crocheted into a lacy openwork panel. By Bonnie Meltzer.*

9-27. *A tree grows from a fuzzy-yarn earth in another of Bonnie Meltzer's bibs. The bibs slip over the neck and tie around the waist, giving a perfect fit to every size.*

years, she is finally using them. A current work is called "The Railway Clerk's Picnic"—another combination of her skills and the antique buttons. Ruth keeps her tongue in her cheek most of the time.

TENT

Catherine Gibson, inspired by a 2½-year-old granddaughter, made the "Meditation Pad" in Figure 9-36. Fortunately for her, a pants factory went broke, and after buying the fabrics at auction, she felt she had to make some use of them. To construct the "Pad," Mrs. Gibson patched squares, padded them lightly with Superfluff, and stitched on the seams. The roof was made from pie-shaped wedges. A small hole was left in the center for a suspension cord, which was anchored with a plastic coffee-can lid. The plastic cover lifts the tent roof. Neoprene sanitary piping was drawn into a circle and used around the roof line to hold the whole thing rigid. The ends of the pipe were anchored with a cork. A hula hoop could probably be substituted for the piping.

9-28

9-29

9-28. "Overnight Case." What was once an old case is transformed into a fantasy with feathers. If the overnight case is so exotic, one can only imagine what the night itself will be like! By Joanna Gray.

9-29. "Blue-Jeans Bag." A worn pair of blue jeans with legs cut off makes a good roomy bag. Shoulder strap is made from the leg, and pockets are all left intact to hold car keys, parking tickets, grocery lists, or change. By Carol Martin, San Diego, Calif.

9-30. Nap Sack. A crocheted hood, with a long train, keeps you warm while napping. The hood filters the sun out of your eyes and keeps drafts off the back of your neck. For indoors or out. By Mark D. Law.

9-31. "Umbrella." Mark Law crocheted a beautifully lacy pattern over an old umbrella frame. Light filters through the yarns to make a delicate pattern on the ground. It is better suited for a sun-brella, of course, than for a rain-brella.

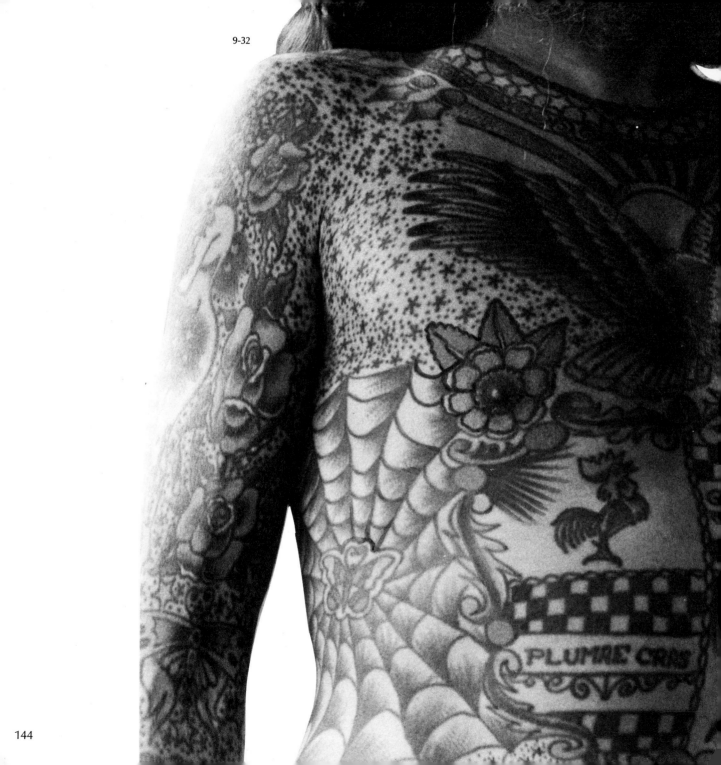

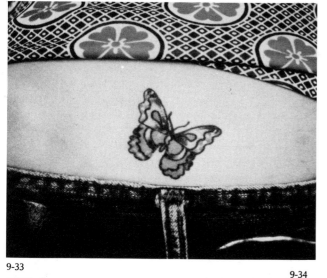

9-33

9-34

9-35

9-32. Lyle Tuttle, a tattoo expert and artist, is himself a beautiful advertisement for this intriguing form of body covering.

9-33. Tattoo on the tummy. By Lyle Tuttle, Los Angeles.

9-34. Another butterfly, in perpetual rest, needle-drawn by Lyle Tuttle.

9-35. Tuttle's tattooed torso.

TATTOOS

When throwaway apparel and recycled clothes are in, it is interesting to see tattooing becoming very popular. The indelible nature of a tattoo involves a commitment which we are not used to recognizing

9-36

9-37

in most body coverings. Certainly this permanent body jewelry does relate to and moves with the skin. While tattoos may not be warming in a physical sense, they offer a visual warmth and cover. Figures 9-32 and 35 show Lyle Tuttle's torso literally encased in a rich linear pattern, with areas of solid color and lettering. He has become a mobile gallery, exhibiting the work of many different tattoo artists. Lyle Tuttle is a nationally recognized master in his field. Some of his tattoos for other people appear in Figures 9-33 and 34.

MASKS
Perhaps in seeking self-identity, hiding one's identity completely plays an important role. If you have ever crawled into a body mask, you are aware of how liberating the experience is. A group encounter in a group mask offers various possibilities! See Figures 9-38 and 41.

Sas Colby's masks raise many questions and open new directions. Wearing a mask makes you challenge many of your own assumptions about yourself. Going beyond the psychology of wearing masks, and the releasing nature of their use, Sas also designs with a great sense of color, pattern, scale, and relief. She is aware of the human form and is as ready to play with it, or poke fun at it, as she is to take it seriously. The masks are beautiful, sensual (though not identifying with either sex), and irresistible. Children love them, which is a pretty good recommendation. Other body masks can be seen in Figures C-5 (Frontispiece) and C-38 (page 56)

9-36. "Katie Kelly's Meditation Pad." This stuffed and patched "tent" covers the body when you want to be alone! Everybody needs a little privacy—especially children. By Catherine Gibson, San Rafael, Calif.

9-37. Dorothy Smaller attached waxed linen thread to a metal collar by Kelly Miller to make this handsome neck piece. Interwoven are I Ching coins and Victorian amber glass.

9-38. "Body Mask for Five." Stitched, with perforations for eyes and mouth, these body masks await the arrival of bodies to animate them. The anonymity of the wearers would have a liberating effect on the conversation or the dancing of the parts of this composite body. By Sas Colby.

9-39. Captivated by the thought of tattooing as body covering, Jo Diggs did this stitchery portrayal of necklace, bracelets, and tattoos.

9-40. Felt "Elephant" mask; satin "Blue Max" mask; satin "Worried Bride" mask; felt "Zipper Mouth" mask. By Sas Colby.

9-41. "Yield"—mask for two. Cotton appliqué on muslin with zippers. By Sas Colby.

9-42. "We Could Make Believe, or We Could be Real"; "Take Off Your Mask Reveal Yourself." Muslin mask for two by Sas Colby.

9-43. *Temporary tattoo. The painted face of Laura Troy.*

9-44. *A body ornament by an anonymous sun-lover.*

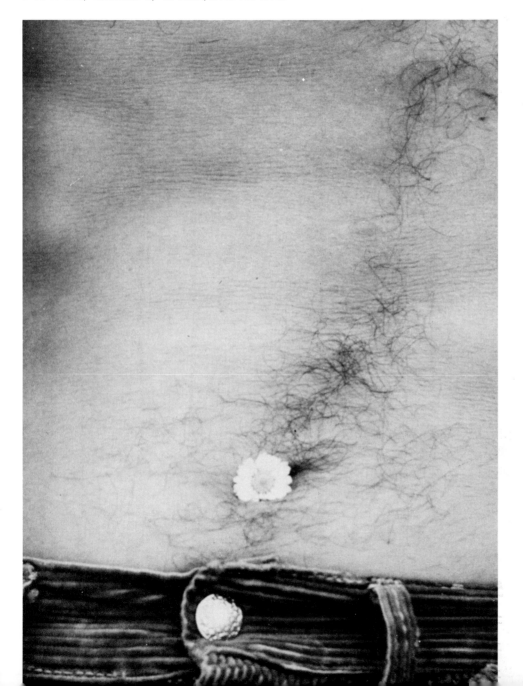

Photo Credits

Joyce Aiken: C-26, 1-7, 2-27, 5-2, 5-3, 5-4, 6-20, 8-15, 9-5, 9-19, 9-29.

Bob Ayre: C-15, 4-35.

Stan Bitters: C-73, C-74, I-4, I-5, I-6, 1-33, 2-4, 2-5, 3-32, 4-25, 7-2, 8-24.

Maggie Brosnan: 3-33.

Ed Caraeff: 3-30, 3-31.

Candace Crockett: 3-12, 3-13, 3-14, 3-16, 3-19, 3-20.

Lenore Davis: 2-25, 2-26.

Jo Diggs: 4-24, 4-36, 8-27, 9-39.

Robert Dvorak: C-11.

Alfred Fisher: C-37, C-38, C-39, C-49, 4-40.

K. Y. Fung: I-2.

Sally Garoutte: 8-4.

Capt. C. Gibson: 9-36.

Joanna Gray: 9-10.

Phyllis Hall: 1-13, 1-28, 1-30, 3-15, 8-20.

Harold B. Helwig: C-41, C-91.

Larry Kuban: 9-23.

Jean Ray Laury: 4-27, 6-6, 7-13, 9-12.

Jeanette Melnick: 2-15.

Paul Miller: C-54, 3-22, 3-23, 3-25, 3-26, 3-27, 9-25.

Gloria McNutt: 4-21.

Kristi O'Neal: 4-32.

Charlotte Patera: C-24, C-42, 9-21.

Jan Simpson: C-25.

Gayle Smalley: C-57, C-58, C-61, C-65, C-66, C-67, C-82, C-86, I-3, 1-1, 1-2, 1-5, 1-6, 1-9, 1-12, 1-21, 1-26, 1-27, 1-32, 1-35, 1-36, 2-19, 2-21, 4-10, 4-17, 4-19, 4-20, 4-34, 4-39, 5-9, 5-11, 6-11, 6-12, 6-13, 6-14, 8-9, 8-10, 8-12, 8-21, 8-22, 9-16, 9-17.

Valerie Harms Sheehan: 4-16, 4-18, 4-38, 9-38, 9-40, 9-41, 9-42.

Lars Speyer: C-35, C-36, C-77, C-78, 2-28.

E. K. Sturgeon: 3-3.

Mike Tilden: 1-34.

Lyle Tuttle: 9-33, 9-34.

Margaret Vaile: 4-29, 8-2, 8-3.

List of Models

Howard Aiken
Jim Aiken
Joel Aiken
Joyce Aiken
Terry Allen
Bets Barnard
Priscilla Beeching
Becky Biller
Bryn Bishop
Jenny Bishop
Marilyn Bishop
Stan Bitters
Roxie Bogner
Lance Bowen
Elsa Brown
Steven Burke
Judy Calandra
Clark Carr
Katherine Marie Carroll
Christalene
Sas Colby
Ralph Colby
Barbara Cutts
Lenore Davis
Jo Diggs
Jack Dunstan
Phyllis Dunstan
Jessica Dvorak
Dodo Folkerts
John Fox
Elizabeth Freeman
Phoebe Fuller
Simone Gad
John Garrett
Joanna Gray
Maja Hahn
Marnie Hall
Patti Handley
Doug Hansen
Dale Janzen
John Jensen
Marjorie Ryall Johnson
William Cahill Johnson
Phillip Kimble
Pennye Kurtela
Bruno La Vergiere
Cay Lang
Beverly Larsen
Frank Laury
Jean Ray Laury
Liz Laury
Tom Laury
Alison Law

Hilary Law
Mark Law
Ruth Law
Fran Levine
Lightfield Lewis
Bridget Maier
K. Lee Manuel
Chris Manuto
Carol Martin
Mason
Jenny Masterson
Jan McAweeney
Gabriella McMillen
Lynn Meyers
Cyndi Miller
Margaret Miller
Barbara Molnar
Louise Murphy
Phyllis Neufeld
Charlotte Patera
Barbara Setsu Pickett
Burdette Pickett
Suzanne Porcella
Yvonne Porcella
Patti Rague
John Reyburn
John Robinson
Don Rose
Jeri Rose
Marion Rose
Patti Rose